GET OUT!
Save Your Life

GET OUT!
Save Your Life
I Did!

Tami Keele

BALBOA.
PRESS

A DIVISION OF HAY HOUSE

Balboa Press books may be ordered through booksellers or by contacting:

Balboa Press
A Division of Hay House
1663 Liberty Drive
Bloomington, IN 47403
www.balboapress.com
1-(877) 407-4847

Because of the dynamic nature of the Internet, any web addresses or links contained in this book may have changed since publication and may no longer be valid. The views expressed in this work are solely those of the author and do not necessarily reflect the views of the publisher, and the publisher hereby disclaims any responsibility for them.

The author of this book does not dispense medical advice or prescribe the use of any technique as a form of treatment for physical, emotional, or medical problems without the advice of a physician, either directly or indirectly. The intent of the author is only to offer information of a general nature to help you in your quest for emotional and spiritual well-being. In the event you use any of the information in this book for yourself, which is your constitutional right, the author and the publisher assume no responsibility for your actions.

Any people depicted in stock imagery provided by Thinkstock are models, and such images are being used for illustrative purposes only.
Certain stock imagery © Thinkstock.

ISBN: 978-1-4525-3391-9 (sc)
ISBN: 978-1-4525-3392-6 (e)

Library of Congress Control Number: 2011905758

Printed in the United States of America

Balboa Press rev. date: 4/29/2011

This book is dedicated to:
My mother Helen Ames,
who is in Heaven with God,
Jesus and all the Angels.
You were my best friend and hero.
This one is for you.

God my Father, Jesus my Savior,
and all the Angels who never left me.

And to everyone that is or has been a victim
of domestic violence in any form.

Special Thanks To:

God, Jesus, and all of the Divine Intervention

Jan L. my Victim's Advocate

Howard and Carole Kohn
Two genuine people that exemplify the word family and
unconditional love. Thank you both for being so real and such
examples of love that is true, pure, honest and never judgmental and
never abandoning me. You're the parents and family I wish I had!

Garret Keele, my Husband & Best Friend

And all of you along the way!
You know who you are!

Contents

Introduction

It is very important to me that this book, the secret that I had lived for eighteen years is interpreted with an open mind and heart. I will take you through the tragic, the triumphant moments and the struggles in my life. There are events and wrongs that happened to me that will also be told. This book takes you down my personal experiences with addiction that my abuser forced upon me.

My book is complete truth. I did my best to relive and recount the trauma from the abuser. However, I was only able to back into it to a point. My Post Traumatic Stress Disorder is now a part of my life and the traumatic damage, my psyche will only allow me to go under the surface. There is a lot I'm not able to talk about still inside of me. My memories continue to thaw; they have been frozen in time. One person can only take so much; I have had more than enough!

The question I get asked quite often is: "Why did you stay so long?"

What most people don't understand is how hard a question it is that they are asking. It is not as simple to walk away from an abusive spouse as they think. Unless they have experienced it for themselves, they do not know the emotions a person goes through with abuse. A victim is torn by these emotions. There is a form of love that is there and it is hard to turn away from what feels like love. There is betrayal and confusion as to why this is happening. This is usually what an abuser depends on, making the victim feel that they are part of the problem. It is a complicated question to answer, but I will answer it very truthfully.

It is my belief that to be an example of any kind, it takes an undying faith and strength that cannot be measured by time. If the experience had been easy, I would not have learned the lessons that were being taught to me. If the road had no speed bumps or sinkholes, I would have never fallen in and learned how to Get Out! I feel as though I have truly fought my way back from the dead a few times over. To make a difference in the world, you must be the example that you want to see. I chose to rise from the ruins of my abused life and begin to find the pieces and put them back together and try to make sense out of the madness. I had to take it upon myself to break the vicious cycle of abuse in my own life and break the chain of abuse in my family. From the wreckage of my life came a re-birth of myself. All alone with no one to rescue me, I learned what total aloneness was.

God tested my faith. It is an easy thing to talk of faith, but to walk by faith is a hard thing to do. You must really believe and I do! Through a very hard lesson of faith I began to walk by faith even when I couldn't see what was ahead or in store for me. I began to walk the walk and talk the talk of my faith and it guided me through the path of life.

There were many times that I wondered if I had done the right thing by getting out. Freeing myself of the chains that binded my life and spirit for so long was the best thing that I have ever done for myself. I showed God and myself that I loved myself enough to not only save my life, but also to love others and help them by telling my story of abuse.

Through my story, I ask that you don't form an opinion until you read the entire book. The message I took from my experience of being alone is that we are never really alone. As long as we have our faith, we always have God, Jesus and all the angels and an abundance of spiritual guidance. Look around your own life and see all that you are blessed with parents, a spouse, children, friends, and animals. Your world is not empty, it is filled with blessings that we often over look. Appreciate all that God has blessed you with. Remember it can be worse and be happy for what is around you as it may not always be there. Give all the love you can and receive love eternally.

Thank you,

Much love,

Tami

Chapter 1
Childhood

During my life I have suffered hardships and abuses by the ones I trusted most. I wish to tell you my story with hope that it will enable others to avoid what has happened to me. This will be a true account of what has happened to me and the details will be as graphic as possible.

I was born in California in 1964. My parents were married for 25 years. They had five children together, two boys and three girls. I am the youngest of the children. My eldest brother is 18 years older than me, because of our age difference I never felt connected to my siblings. I was closer to my nieces and nephews because we were closer in age. My older sister Pam was the closest in age to me being seven years my senior.

At age three I was in a serious car accident. My sister-in-law was driving the car with me in the back seat on my mothers lap. There was no seatbelt or other safety device holding me safely in place, as they were not required at that time. She ran a red light and hit another car and I went through the windshield. My left arm was partially torn off and I also suffered a broken arm, shoulder bone, and collarbone. It required 150 stitches to put my arm back on. I was lucky that my arm was not amputated at the shoulder. For three months I was in the hospital with my arm held up at all times. Before the accident I was left-handed and as a result of the crash I had to learn how to do everything with my right hand. My left arm is still much weaker than my right. I received a settlement and the judge ordered that the money be put into a trust fund until I was 18 years old.

As far back as I can remember I do not think my father ever gave me any affection. My father was an alcoholic and would always be drinking. When he drank he would be physically and mentally abusive towards my mother and me. I remember he would pull me by my long hair across the house and into my room where he would beat me. He did not care that my arm was healing he would beat me anyway. Being a young child I needed love and guidance, not abuse. I don't think I did anything wrong to get this abuse. I would get beat by him with his hand and belt for no reason at all. My mother would be outside the room or down the hall unable to help me for the fear she would get beat herself. My mother was afraid of him, but still she should have stopped him and protected her daughter from his abuse. But because of her fear of him, she chose not to help me. I was a fragile little girl that wanted to be loved by my father, but all he gave me was his anger. As far back as I can remember my father never sat down and had a father/daughter conversation with me. Most fathers take their children to a park to play, to a movie or anything to bond with their child, my father never did any of this or any other activities with me. For some reason I could not understand, he hated me and I hated him for the way he treated me. Painting was the only thing that made me happy, it was an escape from the abuse my father put on my mother and me.

As a child, I was skinny. I was always getting sick from the food I was forced to eat. Several times a week we would go out to a restaurant, it was always the same place. My father would make me eat frog legs, which I do not like but I had no choice, it was frog legs or nothing. When my mother would cook at home, but he would always put things into the food that made it impossible to eat. One time I remember he poured some Coke into the eggs she was cooking. Once a week he made my mother cook Brussels sprouts. I did not like them but I would have to eat them until I got sick and thru up.

I feel that my father was an evil man or that he just did not like us. He would do mean things that I still do not understand why. On several

occasions he would ask us if we wanted to go for ice cream and of course we said "yes". When we got to the ice cream place he would jerk the car around really hard and step on the gas while laughing. My parents would than get into a fight and he would start cussing and slapping her in the face. When we would get home he would tear the house apart. Than he would beat my mother until it was my turn. When he was done I had red welts all over my body. My father was a sick man. I know in my heart that he had to have many mental problems because I never could understand why he hated me.

My childhood was sad and lonely. There were very few happy times that I can remember. One happy memory I can remember is with my friend Denise from kindergarten. She would invite me to spend the night at her house. I always enjoyed spending time there. They had a happy loving family that I wished I had. Every night at dinnertime Denise's mother would cook a nice home cooked meal and everyone would sit at the table and talk about their day. It was what I wished my father had done with me. Every time I would be there I would wish it were my family. When I stayed at her house, I knew that I would not have to listen to the screaming and yelling of my father or the cries of my mother as she was being beaten up.

During one of my parent's fights, he tore the house apart and began beating my mother. I was hiding in the corner behind the door hoping that he would stop, but knew my turn was coming next. He than left the room and returned quickly with his gun. He was yelling at the top of his lungs then he took a shot at my mother. The bullet grazed her head and lodged into the wall. I was terrified. I had never seen him get to that point before. I do not know or understand why she did not leave him then.

This childhood abuse went on for several years until one night on my birthday. My father had tore up the entire house again and beat up my mother. He dragged me by my hair into my room to beat me. I was screaming for someone to help me and prayed that help would come and save me from his hand. My prayers were answered as my eldest brother Ronnie came home to visit. He was surprised and very angry to see that my mother was still allowing the abuse to continue. He picked up the iron, burst into my room and hit my father in the head, which knocked him out. He than took my hand and lead me out of the room. I was traumatized and relieved to get out! Ronnie was very upset; he told my mother that if she did not leave him he was going to call the police. He advised her that if the police came and she had not left, the police would remove the children from the abusive household. My mother agreed and they called the police. The police advised my mother that they were on their way to arrest my father. Ronnie instructed us to go to the car and wait. While he waited in the house to make sure he did not wake up and to wait for the police. After the police arrived, Ronnie took us to my other brother Richards house. We were going to stay with him and his family until my mother could get on her feet.

I remember looking out the window of the car while we were driving to Richards house. There was a police helicopter above us and I could see it lighting up the road in front of us. The police were escorting us to safety, as my mother was afraid some of my father's friends would follow us. It gave me a warm feeling, like God was leading us to a happier life.

My father was a very evil man to abuse us as he did. The abuse was not just directed at my mother and myself; my father was also abusive towards my older siblings as well. From what I understand I was lucky. After my mother left my father she did a lot to protect us. She filed for divorce and we changed our last name. We moved to a different area so that he would not be able to find us. My father spent eight years in prison for domestic violence and child abuse. While in prison, he would call my sisters house and make threats on us. He said that he was going to kidnap me, and that he would kill my mother. A few weeks after his release from prison, he was involved in a car accident. They told me he had a heart attack and died at the scene. I feel that God took this evil man away so that he couldn't hurt anyone ever again. As crazy as it sounds I finally had a sense of release. I felt like I would never have to look over my shoulder in fear of him.

My mother told me that her father never showed her much affection and she just wanted to be loved by him. Because of the relationship she had with her father she became very submissive and dependent on my father to take care of everything. I always told myself that I would never let a man control me or become dependant on someone else. Now that we were on our own, my mother needed to learn how to be independent. She even had to learn how to drive a car as she had always taken the bus before. I was six years old when my mother divorced my father. We were constantly moving from place to place as my mother tried to find a good job. She was working long hours to support us and sometimes I would have to go to work with her and sit there for eight hours. Other times I would be home with my sister Pam or I would be alone.

When I was in the third grade my sister Pam was supposed to watch me until my mother came home from work. Pam would go out with her friends and leave me on my own or she would make me stay in the house. I could see my friends outside playing however I was not allowed to go outside and play with them. Pam had a mean temper like my father.

We lived about a mile from my school and I would have to walk home by myself. It was to far for a seven-year-old child to walk by herself. One day I was walking home from school and noticed I was being followed. It was a boy from the sixth grade. I was scared and began walking as fast as I could. When I finally got home I was out of breath. My hands were shaking and it seemed like I would never get the key in the door. I finally opened the door and went inside locking the door behind me. My mother was working and Pam was out, I was home alone. He started banging on the door and saying "Let me in, I'm coming in." I ran to my bedroom closet and hid. My heart was pounding with fear as I huddled in my closet. This seemed to go on for an hour before he finally left. My mother came home some time later to find me shaken and traumatized. The next day my mother went to school with me to make sure this would not happen again. The boy was expelled from the school and I never heard of him again. It was incidents like this that I might not have suffered if I had my father. I felt like I needed his love and protection. It was not easy growing up without a father, I missed out on the love and guidance that a child needs from her father.

Around this time I began to go to bible study by myself. My mother arraigned for the church bus to pick me up, as my mother had to work and could not take me. This is when I began to call Jesus my father. I was yearning for love and looked to Jesus for guidance and comfort. The church gave me a blue bible for which I still hold very dear to my heart and always will.

When I was nine years old, my mother took Pam and me to the Ice Arena to watch skating. I instantly fell in love with skating. I had to try it. When I first went skating, I knew that it would become a part of me. The smell of the ice was so fresh and clean. The feel of the blades on my skates gliding peacefully across the ice gave me a sense of freedom I had never felt before. I found my inner peace, I felt like I could fly. Skating was a way for me to finally express myself and forget about my troubles both past and present. My mother arranged for me to take lessons and for once in my life I felt like I was alive. I had a feeling as if I had no worries in the world. I was very grateful to my mother for the skating lessons. We were very poor and we could not afford skating outfits. My mother made my outfits by hand, which made me feel loved.

In eighth grade I started going to school at Valley Professional Theater of Performing Arts. This school is where a lot of child actors went. I was not a child actor and it was expensive. So my mother had to use some of my trust fund money to pay for this school. I went to this school so that I could continue to pursue my passion: skating. I would be on the ice at 4 a.m. and skate until 11 a.m. Then I would go to school classes from 12 until 3 p.m. daily. I took the basic courses in school so that my main focus was on skating. I loved this school as it allowed me to skate and get my schooling. Skating and this school kept me isolated from other things that could have influenced me in bad ways such as drugs and alcohol. There was no time in my schedule for getting into trouble. The friends I had at this school basically had the same schedule as I did which was good. I went to this school for eighth and ninth grade. In the ninth grade I began to feel isolated from my friends. They began to ignore me, leaving me out of their activities. I felt so uncomfortable that I did not want to go to that school anymore. Pam and her children lived in Las Vegas and I told my mother that I wanted to move to Las Vegas also.

My mother liked the idea of moving to Las Vegas. She was tired of working hard and getting very little. It was too expensive to live in California. She was working at a restaurant at Universal Studios at this time and asked Telly Sevalas if he could help her get a job in Las Vegas. He got her a job in a restaurant at Caesars Palace. We left California for a new beginning in Las Vegas.

Chapter 2
A New Beginning

With my mother having a job in Las Vegas, we used some of my trust fund money to get there and start in a new beginning in our lives. Using some of the trust fund money was the only way we could've afforded to move. I was fifteen and looking forward to starting a new chapter in my life.

Living in Las Vegas was hard at first. My mother had to work a lot and was gone most of the time. I was home alone and felt like I could do whatever I wanted. Skating was still my passion so every opportunity I had to skate I did. My coach from California moved to Las Vegas just before we did and I was taking a few lessons a week from her. Being able to skate with her made me feel comfortable even though I felt out of place. It helped me get adjusted to my new surroundings. I missed the friends I left in California, but started to make new ones. At first it was very hard to make new friends because I was not used to being in a big public school.

When I turned sixteen years old I was getting pressured by my mother to get a job to help out with expenses. Ever since I started skating I dreamed of being up on stage skating in a big ice skating show. There was a show at the Hacienda Hotel and Casino called Ice Fantasy. I called and was able to talk to the producer Ron Andrews and we set up an audition. It was a big deal since twenty-one was the minimum age to be in a show. I was extremely excited and nervous all in one. I could not believe that I had lined up this audition. I prayed to Jesus to help me get this job. Being my first job interview I did not want to go alone, so my mother and sister-in-law went to the audition with me. We met with Ron and the line captain for the show. After skating for a few minutes they called me over to talk to them. They asked me to model for them and I did, than they wanted me to model topless for them and my mother was shocked. She said "Oh God" and started to walk away. I asked my mother and sister-in-law to leave the room. I removed my top and they told me I had beautiful breasts. The feeling that gave me was incredible, I was proud and felt like I could walk on water. They offered me a full-time skater position for which I joyfully accepted.

I began to learn my moves for the show and was fitted for my costumes. This job was a dream come true for me. It was both hard and exciting for me but was well worth it. I skated two shows a night and was getting home at 2 in the morning. Not having time for both work and school, I had to drop out of school and get my GED. This show was my job for two years until the show closed down.

At seventeen I began dating and had a terrible taste in boys. They were all wrong for me, but at that age I was rebellious. Mike was my first love and my mother hated him. He was quite abusive to me. He lied, cheated, and slapped me around. I was stupid for staying with a boyfriend that was abusive, but thought I was in love.

After my eighteenth birthday I was going to go get what was left of my trust fund money from my accident at age three. My mother wanted me to wait, but I was in a hurry to get my money. We made plans to go on Friday the thirteenth. Mike was going to drive me to California to get it. First, we went to Disneyland and he seemed to be distant from me. He was not nice to me and was very irritable. I should have known something was wrong, but I tried to have fun anyway. At about eleven p.m. we left and we started driving back to our hotel. He wasn't talking to me in the car until about ten minutes into our ride. We were on the Santa Ana Freeway in Anaheim and he told me that he wanted some of my money. I told him that it was my money and not his. He did not like that and got really mad. He told me that my passbook was locked in his glove box and he was going to the bank by himself and taking all of my money. I could not believe what I was hearing. I began panicking and tried to get the glove box open, but I couldn't open it. He punched me in the face and lost control of the car. The car crashed into the center embankment and spun around coming to rest facing the wrong way on the freeway. He told me to get out of the car, but I was dazed and in shock and couldn't move. He opened his door and ran to the side of the freeway leaving me in the car. Finally, I regained my bearings, opened the car door and began to get out. Just then another car hit me head on. I hit the dashboard and flew out and over the car landing face down on the freeway. My skull was fractured and was bleeding in the brain. One of the witnesses to the accident was a nurse that worked at a nearby hospital in Anaheim. She held my head and kept me covered until the ambulance arrived. I was going in and out of consciousness as I laid there on the freeway. If not for her, I would not be here today.

When the police and ambulance arrived, Mike told the police that I caused the accident by hitting him and that made him lose control of the car. With me being treated on the freeway, I could not tell the police what really had happened. I was quickly loaded in the ambulance and rushed to Anaheim Memorial Hospital. Mike rode in the front of the ambulance with me since his car was totaled.

When I arrived at the hospital, I was barely conscious. I remember hearing Mike tell the emergency room nurses that I was high on drugs and was tripping out. They knew that I had just been in an accident, but they believed him and left me in the hallway. I believe that he wanted me to die so that the truth about what had happened in the car would never come out as he had been arrested several times before. Plus, he would then be able to get my money from the bank. At the hospital, Mike called his parents who immediately flew there to take care of things. It was them that made Mike call my mother.

As I lay in the hallway, my condition worsened. A doctor was walking by just as I leaned over and threw up blood right in front of him. He said, "Oh God! She's in trouble!" I was immediately rushed to the ICU in the pediatrics ward. The doctors began to do everything that they could to control my bleeding. Once I stabilized they began to run tests to see how bad my brain injury was. My skull was fractured and I had a hema toma of the right side of my brain, which formed a blood clot. They determined that because of where the blood clot was that if they operated it would kill me. They had to just let my brain heal itself. My chances for survival were not good. My mother arrived at the hospital with my sister Pam the next day and brought me a little bouquet of yellow silk flowers. They were only able to stay for two days as she had to get back to work or lose her job. While there, she went to Mike's car and was able to retrieve my passbook.

I was in and out of a coma for three days while I was in the intensive care unit. They than moved me to a private room for four more days. I almost died and I know it was Jesus that saved my life. My mother told me that she put my life in God's hands and she could no longer help me. However, she was wrong. I still needed her love and affection for which she didn't give me. The best thing she could have done for me would have been to put her arms around me, hold me and tell me that she loved me. My mother wasn't very nurturing to me. The nurse from the freeway was one of my nurses in the hospital, she along with the other nurses in my area felt sorry for me not having anybody to visit me. They would come in and talk to me quite often. It was nice to know that someone cared about me.

After a week in the hospital, my mother was called back to the hospital to take me home. The doctors told her that I needed to fly home because the drive from Los Angeles to Las Vegas would kill me. She was not happy, but she flew to California to get me and bring me home. I remember my head was pounding as I was being moved into the airplane. My head was in a big brace so that it wouldn't move around. The doctors told me to go home and stay in bed, as my brain needed time to heal. When we got home my mother put me to bed.

The next morning I woke up and thought I felt pretty good. Wanting to take a real shower, I got up and into the shower. That was a big mistake. I began to feel dizzy as I was looking up at the shower nozzle and that was it. At that point, I had a seizure. My mother heard me scream and came in to find me passed out at the bottom of the shower. Thank God my mother heard me scream or I might have drowned or died.

I woke up in the emergency room at Sunrise Hospital. After they were sure I was stable, they admitted me and kept me in the hospital for two weeks to let my brain heal. During my stay, they ran tests on my brain to see if it was healing. The doctors ran brain wave and CAT scans on me several times. They thought I might not ever fully recover it was touch and go at that point.

When I was released and told again to get a lot of bed rest I did just that. I was lying down almost all day, as my head was still very heavy. Once a week I would go to see my neurosurgeon, other than that I did almost nothing for about three months.

After my recovery I began to take life very slow. My head was still very fragile, the doctors told me that if I get hit in the head that might be the end for me and I need to be extremely careful with my head for the rest of my life. With almost losing my life I wanted to enjoy what I almost lost. I told myself that I was going to try new and different things. I was going to do things that I thought would be fun and create great memories that would last a lifetime.

Before my accident, I worked for a modeling agency and they would send me out for many different modeling jobs. There were some photo shoots, but mostly I would work as a model for conventions that were in town. There was a lot going for me being young and pretty. After the Ice Fantasy show closed, I tried working several different jobs to find what I wanted to do. Living in Las Vegas there were many hotel/casinos where I could get a job. I tried everything I thought would be interesting. I was a cashier at a restaurant, hotel front desk clerk, and player's club attendant. Those jobs were not for me, but they were interesting and paid the bills. My life finally seemed to be going good for me. I wanted to go to beauty school but knew I was not ready.

Three years went by and I began working at the Golden Nugget as a cocktail server on the casino floor and was then moved into the lounge. I really loved my job. I was making great money and was able to meet all kinds of people. While working in the lounge I made friends with some of the hotel guests. I did the cover of the Las Vegan magazine promoting the Golden Nugget. Steve Wynn owned the Golden Nugget at this time and would come into the lounge often. There was a soap opera that Steve Wynn's sister-in-law was doing from the lounge that I was working in and I had a small part. This was a good time in my life and I was having the time of my life. I began to search for love and couldn't find what I needed. I was meeting all the wrong ones, but was still waiting for my true love to come and find me. I knew that there was someone out there for me to love and someday they would walk into my life and I would have everything I wanted in life. God put somebody on this planet for me and I had faith that they would find me.

While working in the lounge I met a real nice man. When he first came on to me I told him that I just wanted to be friends. He seemed to be all right with that, but he did not get it. He would send me flowers at work everyday, then at home. Each bouquet would be a different color, but mostly I received bouquets of red roses. One day he flew me to California to have lunch with him. After lunch he gave me an envelope and told me not to open it until I got back to Las Vegas. When I returned home I opened the envelope and it had eleven thousand dollars in it with a note. The note said for me to use the money to buy a car, which I did. I bought a new red Rally Sport Camero Z-28 with t-tops. He wanted me to buy a car because he knew I did not have one and was always using my mother's. He was a very generous man. He cared about me and kept saying things like maybe you will fall in love with me. But I did not have those kinds of feelings for him and I kept telling him we could only be friends. All of my other friends were telling me to be with him and that he was perfect for me, but my heart was not in it. I didn't want to be with someone because they were wealthy. It was important for me to be in love with the person I was with. My faith kept me believing that I would find someone, fall in love and have a real relationship.

Chapter 3
Falling For A Lie

On my way home from work one evening I stopped to get something to eat at a fast food restaurant as I normally did. This time was quite different. I met a man on the way out named was Steven. He was just my type, tall, handsome and muscular. My heart was pounding with anticipation, it felt like love at first sight. We sat in my car and talked for quite a while. I offered him my phone number and said, "I don't call guys, they call me!" He told me he would call me the next day.

I was up all night in anticipation waiting for his call. The sun finally rose above the horizon and my excitement grew, as it wouldn't be long before his call. Finally at about noon the phone rang and it was him. We talked for some time and it felt like we were old friends. As we talked we got to know each other pretty well. He was from California and was in Las Vegas visiting some old friends. He told me he had spent the last four years in the marines and was now looking for a job. He was twenty-seven years old, which was about five years older than me. He was into fast cars, hard rock music, and liked to drink and smoke. I wasn't interested in anything that he was into. I was falling for a lust.

He hated almost everything about my life and the fact that I had a lot going for me. He didn't like that I was a professional skater, model, and most of all a cocktail waitress. The only thing he liked was that I was very pretty. This should've been enough for me to walk away, but he was my type of man. We really had nothing in common other than physical attraction. This relationship was all wrong from the start.

Look Inside

Beautiful life, beautiful world
Peace and Love
Beautiful people everywhere
Take off the mask
Look inside
Find yourself
Thank God that you're alive
Forget the past
You can't change it
Don't look back
Look inside

You will find the God in you
Beautiful life, beautiful world
Peace and Love
Harmony on Mother Earth
Feel the grass
Don't just pass
Look at the trees
They're talking to you
They're talking to me
Be yourself
Look inside
It will make you better
Just do your thing
Go and sing
Just be if it makes you feel better
Just do your thing
Dance, Dance to the music
Look inside
Free yourself and just be
If it makes you feel better
Cleanse your soul
Stop the pity party that gets old
Clear your soul
Don't let life pass you by
It's ok to cry
Look inside
Don't let life pass you by

We began dating and our relationship moved very fast. After being together for about three weeks he wanted to get married. I told him it was too soon. He was becoming very possessive of me. It started with him telling me what I could and couldn't do. He would tell me how beautiful I was, but he would try to hide me from the world. It seemed that none of my friends liked my new boyfriend and they all thought I could do so much better. Even Steven told me I could do better and that he never had a girlfriend as beautiful as me before. There were signs for me to walk away from the start, but we fell hard and fast for each other. It felt like a void in my life was filled by his love for me. I was naïve and thought I had finally found the love of my life.

He began to get a strong grip on my life. After dating for a month he moved into the apartment I was sharing with my mother. My mother said it was ok at first. When she started to get to know him she didn't like him and wanted him out. She thought he was a bum. She would tell me, " He dresses and looks like a bum" and she was quick to point out that he didn't have a job.

He quickly began to take control of my life. He would tell me what I could and couldn't wear. He would tell me which of my friends I could talk to and when. I could no longer talk to my male friends and wasn't allowed to go out with my female friend without him going along with us. My friend tried to tell me to get away from him, but I didn't want to hear her warnings. I was in love with him and nothing else mattered. I should've listened to my friend's warnings about him. As our relationship grew my friends went about their lives. It was my fault for not listening to my friends before my relationship with him got out of control. But when you think you're in love we do stupid things. As time went by he began to treat me as if he owned me.

A few weeks after he moved in I needed to have surgery on my wrist. A cist had formed and needed to be removed. He then began working downtown at The Golden Gate Casino. With him having a job, he told me that he didn't want me to go back to work. He never wanted to see me in my cocktail waitress uniform and hated the fact that other men saw me in my uniform every day. For the man that I was in love with, I quit my job. My mother was furious with me that I quit my job for him. She didn't agree with my decision and thought I was making a big mistake and giving him total control of my life. I knew in my heart I was making a mistake for several reasons. First,

I loved my job, co-workers, and the money was good. Second, by quitting my job it gave him more power over me, as I now needed him to support me. Third, I basically had no one to talk to other than him.

One day he started to talk to me about getting married again. I stated to him that I would never marry a smoker and if he wanted to marry me, he needed to quit. In my opinion, it is a disgusting habit and I wanted no part of it in my life. He became angry and began to drink shots of whiskey one after the other and was getting louder by the minute. He began yelling at me and not liking the way this felt emotionally, I began heading out of the bedroom. He caught me at the top of the stairs, pushed me into the wall preventing me from going downstairs. As I tried to get away he clinched his powerful hands around my arms and squeezed as hard as he could. The pain it caused me was unbearable. His face turned red and he looked like the devil with eyes that could kill. I was terrified and started to cry and begged him to let me go. It felt like an eternity but he finally released his grip on me. He stepped back away from me as he slowly turned and went down the stairs and out to his car. After I composed myself I went to the bathroom and looked in the mirror. His hands left indentations with bruises beginning to form around both of my arms. I could see a perfect impression of his fingers around my throbbing arms. This was a major red flag that I shouldn't have looked past. Thinking back I should've walked away then and saved myself a lot of heartbreak, pain and misery. All I could think about at that moment was how much I hated him.

When I went out to see what he was doing in his car, the doors were locked and he wouldn't let me in. He was sitting in the driver's seat smoking and drinking. I tried to talk to him, but he just ignored me. All he gave me was one pissed off look from the corner of his eye. He ended up falling asleep in his car and spent the night out there. The next few days my arms were hidden so that nobody could see my bruises. Another red flag that I ignored was that he never showed me any remorse for what he did to me. He acted like it never happened.

In The Beginning

In the beginning I believed
In every word you said
You promised me an unconditional love
One that would never leave me
Or hurt me
You promised me a rainbow
Red, Blue, Purple, Green and yellow too!
When you took off your mask
The rainbow you promised
Were the colors I began to wear!
I call that Black and Blue
From your anger and destruction
The bruises became my war wounds
I hid the pain from everyone
No one had a clue
What was underneath my clothes!
My rainbow from you
As you warned me
What you would do to me
If I ever told
In the end I realized
The only rainbow I would get
Was the one that I would create on my own
With my faith never broken
A broken spirit can heal
My spirit survived the hell of your hands
With my hands I prayed
For a new beginning
A second chance at life
In the beginning!

His temper was out of control. One moment he would be nice and loving and the next he would be yelling at me. After he would hurt me he would sometimes try to be real nice and expect me to forget about what he had done and go on with our lives. However, I couldn't forget. The memories of the hell he was putting me through just kept stacking up.

After this violent episode, I put off our wedding for six months. Of course the next six months went by without any type of anger or abuse. He was a perfect gentleman and showed me love. He would open doors for me, write me little love letters and buy me beautiful flowers. However, it was just an act to get me back under his control. He asked me what kind of man I wanted him to be. I told him I needed a man that would never lie to me or hit me, a man that would be there for me and take care of me. I was hoping that this was the beginning of something wonderful, but there was still a bad feeling in my head that he was not the man of my dreams. Unfortunately, my heart was ruling over my head.

We were getting along pretty good, which meant he was probably hiding things from me. Again I informed him that he had to quit smoking before we could get married. He promised me that he had quit and there was nothing to worry about. I now know he was lying about quitting. He just made sure I was not around when he would smoke. When I would smell the smoke on him, he would tell me it was from working in a casino.

He demanded that my car be sold before we could get married. He didn't like that another man bought my car for me. He said that we needed to buy a married car and not a sports car. He sold his car, which was a piece of junk. The air-conditioning was broken and we were living in the hot desert. We traded my car in and bought a 1988 Pontiac Grand-am. It was a nice car, but I enjoyed my Chevy Camero much more. As we only had one car now, I would drive him to work and then pick him up.

He managed to talk me into going forward with our plans to get married. We started to plan a small wedding. My mother didn't approve of us getting married and stated that she didn't want to come. We decided to elope because the cost was becoming too much for us to afford. On

December 23, 1987, we went to the Little White Wedding Chapel dressed in jeans and matching flannel shirts and exchanged our vows with no family or friends there. After our ceremony, we went out and had a nice dinner and a few drinks.

When we arrived back at our apartment, my mother was asleep. I poked my head into her room and told her what we did. She looked at me and said "Oh". As it was no big deal to her as she probably knew I made a big mistake. We then went into our room and he went to sleep. We didn't even have sex on our wedding night as he didn't want to. He said, "We're married now, it doesn't matter when we have sex." That was another sign that I wasn't with the right man. I was lying there next to him in bed staring up at the mirror on the top of my canopy bed wondering what I had just done. He just snored the night away; I probably wouldn't have been able to sleep anyway!

After getting married, we quickly began to look for a home of our own. I was so excited about the new life we were about to start together. Steven wanted a house so that he would have a garage and a yard, as he liked to work on cars. I wanted a condo because I didn't think we could afford a house, and I didn't want to landscape the backyard. In Las Vegas the backyards were just plain dirt and needed to be landscaped. I could just imagine all of that dirt inside the house and wanted no part of that. By getting a condo, there would be a pool, more people around and no dirt to worry about. With me wanting to have people closer to us should have been another sign of trouble.

Within two months of being married, Steven and I found a home we agreed on and bought it. It was a new two-bedroom condo. I was excited about our first home. I began thinking about the color of the carpet and flooring. We picked a forest green carpet. It was pretty, however it wasn't my choice. Green was his favorite color and that was final. The linoleum was my choice and it was white.

It was a new beginning for the two of us and we were trying to make the best of what we had. We began to shop for the things we needed to make our house a home. However, my mother wasn't excited for us. I think she wanted to come with us, as she felt abandoned. She had never been on her own before. Deep down inside I felt guilty for leaving her, but I needed to start a life with my husband. My mother was living her life and we needed to start ours.

We couldn't afford to buy very much in the way of furniture, so the family room and dining room were mostly empty. The only things we had in those rooms were beanbag chairs and a television on a milk crate. Our home felt uncomfortable to me and I spent most of my time either in the bedroom or the kitchen. He came home one day with a .357 revolver. This made me a little angry, as we needed the money for other things. He ignored my complaints, as my opinion didn't matter.

As time went on our marriage became rocky as he was making all of the decisions in our lives without any input from me. I felt as though we should be making the decisions together as a couple. He would say that it was his job to take care of me and I should just trust him to do what was best for both of us. I conceded this argument to him as I knew there was no way he would let me be a part of the decision making and the paying of the bills.

About three months into our marriage, he had surgery for an abdominal hernia. The doctor prescribed him pain pills, which he told me made him feel good. He continued taking the pills even though he didn't need them anymore. When he ran out of his pills, he took the pain pills I had left from my wrist surgery. I saw this as a real problem, but I still loved him and looked the other way. Every time we did something together he would need to take pills. He was becoming addicted to them.

My teeth began hurting me, but having a fear of the dentist, I waited until I could no longer stand the pain. The dentist informed me that my wisdom teeth had become impacted and infected. The dentist prescribed antibiotics and pain pills. This made Steven happy. I would take a pain pill and he would take several. He wouldn't let me have my teeth removed, as this was a way for him to get more pills. He took me to several different dentists, just to get more pills. I was too terrified to say anything as my fear of him was growing.

He began going to the doctor to get his own pain pills. He told the doctor his back was hurting. When I tried to get him to stop taking the pills, he would get very angry. He became violent towards me, yelling at me, calling me horrible names and abusive physically. I would get grabbed by the arms and pushed into walls or slapped and told to "shut up!"

Trying to make things better between us, I would cook his favorite dinner, pot roast with potatoes and carrots. He would come to the table, look at me, the food, then for some reason he would throw the food against the wall and walk away without saying a word. The roast was on the floor and the juice splattered over the wall. All of the time, love and hope that I put into making him dinner was wasted as the dinner was ruined.

This was becoming a life of hell and I hated everything about it. It seemed no matter what I tried to do to make our marriage better, it just kept getting worse. He had total control of my life. I was trapped. All of my friends went about their lives and my family had become distant from me. He never wanted to go to any of my family gatherings, nor would he let me attend. When we did go to family gatherings, he would sit on the couch and watch television, not socializing with anyone. I couldn't tell anyone what was happening to me because I was terrified of what he would do to me.

There were times when he would be nice to me and take me places. One time we flew to California and stayed by the beach. It began as a romantic trip, we had a wonderful candlelight dinner and walked hand in hand on the beach. My heart began to fall in love all over again as this was what I thought a loving relationship would be.

The next day, April 19, 1988, he took me to my favorite place, Disneyland. He was quite different here. One minute he was nice and the next he seemed agitated. I tried to get him to relax and enjoy the day with me, but it was not to be. When we returned to the hotel, we began to argue. He left the hotel and didn't return for about three hours. He probably needed to smoke a cigarette and didn't want me to know he was smoking. When he walked out, I was scared and didn't know what to expect. Was he going to come back or just leave me there? When he returned to the hotel he seemed different. He was quite anxious and quiet. I kept my mouth closed, as I didn't want to escalate anything.

After we returned home, I asked him if he wanted a divorce. He said he didn't and that we were going to be together forever and he would never leave me. As we really had nothing in common, I don't see how he could've been happy. I was living in a life of hell and wanted out, but being dependant on him I had nothing, nowhere to go and was afraid of being alone.

It was then right back to him making me get him pills. It seemed like he enjoyed seeing me suffer so that he could get more pain pills, as that is all he seemed to care about. It had come to the point that I dreaded my life. I hated waking up in the morning. However, I honestly felt that I loved him even though we didn't have enough in common to sustain our marriage. My heart believed he was my soul mate. When we looked into each other's eyes there was a bond that I had never felt before. I would hope and pray he would change and become the man of my dreams. My marriage to him was very important to me. Coming from a divorced family, I was determined to make my marriage work. Even at the lowest point, I never wanted to separate. I truly loved him with all of my heart.

Chapter 4
Losing Myself

Steven began mentally controlling me. He started telling me things to bring down my self-esteem so that he could maintain total control of my life. With me not having anyone around to tell me otherwise, I began to believe his lies. He would tell me that my face was not pretty enough to get another man and that I was lucky to still have him. He would constantly tell me that I was fat and no one wanted to be with a fat woman. When I look back at the pictures of me at this time, I looked pretty good and wasn't fat.

At this time in our marriage, he was heavy into pain pills. It had come to the point that I think he loved the pills more than me. He wanted me to take the pills with him; I guess he felt that if we took them together it might justify him taking them. He would take several and then give me several to take. Not wanting to become addicted to the pills like him and being afraid of what he might do to me if I refused, I pretended to take them and would spit them out as soon as he turned away. I ended up having about a bottle full of pills hidden from him that I spit out. They would end up getting flushed down the toilet when he wasn't around or I would take some if I needed them for the pain in my teeth or from being physically abused by him. It was an everyday habit for him to take pills. He began making me see more Doctors and Dentists using fictitious names so that he could maintain his habit. Not wanting to do it anymore,

I tried to talk to him. He told me I had to do it! I hated doing it for him and knew it was wrong, but what could I do. I was too afraid to say "no."

It was in the beginning of September 1988. We took a trip to California to visit his father. When we arrived there, Steven went into his stepmother's bathroom and took a handful of pills she was taking. I don't know what kind of pills they were or how many he took, but they made him very high. We went out to get something to eat and when we arrived at the restaurant, he didn't seem to know what was going on or where he was. He was very clumsy bumping into almost everybody he walked past. Everyone in the restaurant was starring at us. I was so embarrassed by how he was acting. The pills were probably sedatives because he was losing control of his body and slurring his words. I couldn't wait to get out of there and ended up leaving the restaurant before we ordered our food.

When we left the restaurant, he became belligerent towards me. In the car, he back handed me and slapped me a few times. When the car stopped at a light, I wanted nothing more to do with him and jumped out. I had no idea where I was, but it didn't bother me, as anywhere was better than being with him. When he caught up to me he tried to apologize. I told him to take me home! He agreed, and we went back to his father's house and picked up our things and headed home.

On the drive home, he kept saying demeaning things to me, and calling me a loser and a waste of a human life. He wanted to start a fight with me and I was having no part of it. I just sat there and ignored him. We were almost home when he reached over and grabbed my left hand. I thought for a second that he was going to say something nice to me. To my horror, he began to bend my fingers back and twisted them back and forth. I began to scream in pain and tried to get him to stop, but he wouldn't. When he did let go of my hand I thought my fingers were broken. The pain was unbearable and I couldn't wait to get out of the car. I asked him to take me to the hospital and he agreed. That is probably what he wanted to happen anyway as he probably wanted more pain pills for him. He took me to the Sunrise Hospital to get medical attention.

Luckily, my fingers were not broken, they were badly bruised and my wrist was sprained. They put a light brace on my wrist to keep me from moving it for a few days. Before I was allowed to leave the hospital, the Domestic Violence Counselor's had to talk to me. They made Steven leave the room and go to the waiting room. They told me he was not going to change and my life was not going to get better. I told them that it would be all right, even though deep down I knew it wouldn't get better. They tried to get me to leave him, but I couldn't as I thought I had nowhere to go. But anywhere would've been better than being with him.

After he would hurt me, he would try to be real nice. Flowers and candy would appear on the counter with little notes of his love for me. This went on for a few weeks until he would have another fit of anger. He would try to start fights with me, but not wanting to fight with him, I would keep my mouth shut as much as possible. It seemed to make him become irate. He would go crazy and throw things around and leave our house on foot. He would be gone for two to three days at a time. When he returned home, he was always filthy dirty and reeking of alcohol. He told me he would go out in the desert and drink whiskey until he passed out and slept on the ground. I began to think that he might be bi-polar, as he was nice at times and violent at other times. This behavior would happen about once a month for reasons beyond my control.

Trying to make my marriage manageable, I made him another nice dinner. This time it was another of his favorite dinners, Beef Stroganoff. When he came to eat, it was the same result. Without him saying a word, dinner was thrown against the wall and he just walked away. As I watched the sauce slowly drip down the wall to the floor it felt as though it was me slowly sliding down the wall. It seemed as though a pattern was forming and I couldn't do anything about it.

He began to purchase more guns. He had a collection of several pistols and rifles at this point. He took me out to the desert and taught me how to handle and shoot them. I didn't want anything to do with them, but thought I might need to protect myself from him one day. It was sad, I felt that I might need to protect myself from my husband more than an intruder!

A few months later, we were having another argument about him lying to me about his smoking. No matter what I would do or say to him, he would never tell me the truth. I always told him to just tell me the truth and we would work it out. It was his lying about it that made me hate it even more.

He began to get angry and started yelling at me. At this time my fear started to grow. Trying to walk away from him, I felt a pain in my back again. He had picked up his rifle case and he was hitting me in the lower back with it in a stabbing motion as he pushed me into the wall. I was screaming in pain begging him to stop, but he kept pounding it into my back. Then he tossed the case onto the floor and stormed down the stairs of our condo, jumped into our car and drove away.

Some of our neighbors heard me screaming and called the police. When the police arrived they wanted me to press charges against him. I refused to press charges. The police officer gave me a card for Domestic Violence and told me I should get a divorce before he kills me. They tried to talk some sense into me, but I was too afraid of him.

The next morning, I called my mother and asked her to take me to the hospital. We went to the emergency room at Sunrise Hospital and they did an MRI on my lower back. The test showed that he had ruptured my L4 and L5 disk. They wanted to know how it happened. I told them my husband continuously stabbed his rifle case into my back. They wanted to call the police and get me to press charges. I told them the police had already been there. My mother was furious at me for not putting him in jail. The Domestic Violence Counselor came in to see me and again tried to get me to leave him. But, I couldn't leave him as he had control of everything in my life and for some reason I was still in love with him.

He was gone for two days and when he called to say that he was coming home. I wanted him to see that I was pretty, so I decided to get dressed up. It was hard, as I had been crying since he had left and my eyes were puffy.

When he came home, he stunk bad and was very dirty as if he slept in the desert. As he walked in I was standing there and I began to cry. He looked at me and said, "I'm sorry. I'll never leave you or hit you again. And by the way I want to come clean. I've been lying to you ever since we got married. I never quit smoking!"

I said, "You've been lying straight to my face for a year!" I had been constantly asking him about smoking and he would always tell me the smell was from him working in a casino. He would swear to God and wish that his mother would get cancer if he were lying.

"I'll try to quit smoking, but I can't make you any promises!" he told me.

"You really hurt me," I said to him, "You ruptured my L4 and L5 disks in my back."

He responded, "You're lying. I didn't hurt you that bad."

"Now you have messed me up for the rest of my life. They can't be fixed. I will have to live with this forever. Do you realize what you have done to me?" I cried.

Then he became combative toward me and said, "I didn't do that to you!" Then he continued on by saying "You made me do it, it was your fault!" I knew that it wasn't my fault, but what else could I say to him without setting him off again? So, with that I told him to take a picture of me so that you can see how pretty I am and how bad hurt me.

Nothing else was said about what he had done to me. It was almost like nothing had happened at all. I was terrified of him becoming violent again, so I kept my distance. We only communicated when he said something to me. My answers were short and precise because I didn't want to set him off. The next year went by without much violence towards me. I pretty much kept my distance and was very careful not to set him off in any way.

On my Birthday three years into our marriage, we were going to go back to visit his father for the weekend. I was sitting on the edge of our bed and he came into the room and said "Happy Birthday, Babe." As he walked across the room towards me, I thought he was going to give me a Birthday kiss. Instead, he slapped me across the face so hard that all I saw were stars. I was stunned and in shock as not knowing why he slapped me. I never found out why he hit me.

After being slapped, I was dreading the trip to California. It was my worst Birthday ever. In the car, I didn't say much if anything at all. When he talked to me, I responded to him. That was all as I was afraid of what might happen if anything else came out of my mouth.

When we arrived at his father's house, he again took several of his stepmother's pills. He then went into our room and slept most of the trip. As we were getting ready to come home, he began another fit of anger and pushed me into the door of our room. The doorknob hit me in the middle of my back and I fell to the floor in pain. It was a long and painful drive back home as the pain in my back was unbearable.

We again went to Sunrise Hospital. They brought the Domestic Violence Counselor in to talk to me again. She informed me that they would protect me from him. However, I declined their help. I told her that he had control of everything in my life and I had nowhere to go. She told me that there were resources available to help me. Still, I was too afraid and said " No". She insisted I was making a big mistake that was going to cost me my life. She also told me that a paper trail was being created and soon it would be out of my control. I should have taken her advise at that time. It would have saved me a lot of pain and suffering, both physically and emotionally.

My teeth were in very bad shape and he used my fear of the Dentist to continue his addiction. He allowed my teeth to be neglected as his teeth were well maintained. The money we had set a side for my teeth to be fixed was used to replace his five front teeth instead. However, my wisdom teeth needed to be removed and he tried to get me to have them taken out. He knew that there were many more teeth in my mouth that would continue to get him pain pills.

This one day it was raining outside, I love the rain. Things between us were pretty good at this time and I was waiting for him to get home from work. Dinner was going to be on the table when he walked through the door. When he walked into the condo, I could tell something was not right. I asked him what was wrong and he said "nothing". The aroma of cigarettes was strong so I figured he had been smoking.

In a soft, calm voice I asked him if he had been smoking. He looked at me and the anger in his face was terrifying, his eyes turned red and I could see the veins in his forehead begin to bulge out. Before I could react, he lunged towards me and knocked me to the ground with him coming down on top of me. His left leg landed on top of my right arm and the pain was incredible. I was pinned to the floor. He was yelling and cursing at me as he clinched his strong hands around my neck and began to choke me. Not being able to breath, I tried to get free from him, but it just made him squeeze my neck tighter. When I was about to pass out, he released his grip and got off of me. He was still yelling at me as he walked out the door and left on foot. When I managed to pull myself off the floor, my right arm was numb and hurting badly. I drove to Sunrise Hospital for treatment, as it felt like my arm was broken.

After my examination in the Emergency Room, the Domestic Violence Counselor came in to talk to me. The first thing they saw when they entered the room was the red marks around my neck from his hands. They were upset that I was still too afraid to leave him and at this point for some reason I didn't want to trust anyone. It was sad because they were the ones that I needed to trust.

Never in my wildest dreams did I think I would ever go through what my mother did with my father, but here I was in the same situation as she had been in years before. Even though I always told myself that would never happen to me, here I was. It was as though something came over me I couldn't control. I was young, pretty, a hard worker, and didn't deserve what was happening to me. But somehow I let it happen. There were red flags everywhere and the signs were on the walls and I didn't want to see them.

I don't know what was worse, the physical abuse, mental abuse or his lies. He was a pathological liar. It was as though he couldn't tell me the truth about anything, not even the smallest issues. I had to find out the truth on my own, which made his lies hurt more. For most of the things he was lying about wouldn't have bothered me, but the fact that he needed to lie about them made me scared and annoyed. It was scary because I didn't know what was going on in his head that made him feel that he needed to lie to me. He knew that I didn't want to be with a smoker, but the fact that he was lying about his smoking made it more of an issue. We could've worked it out if he would've told me the truth. Communication is the backbone of any relationship and ours didn't have much, if any at all.

There were times when he would hit or slap me that he tried to fix it immediately. When you have been abused, forgetting the abuse is not an option. He would harass me if I wasn't acting the way he wanted me to act, as if it didn't happen! He would say things such as "Come on, Tam!" or "I didn't mean it", or "I want to have fun with you, just be normal." Unfortunately for me, I really loved him and thought he was my soul mate. The relationship was very toxic, the pills, drinking, and smoking. I thought I was the only person that understood him, but I didn't really know him at all.

Our marriage was extremely troubled, but there were happy times, times when I was treated like his wife. He would open doors for me, ordered my food, pushed in my chair, and other nice things. He would go to the store and buy food and I would cook a nice dinner for the two of us to enjoy. He gave me cards for no reason other than to make me feel loved.

He would take my pills along with the pills he was getting from the doctors he was seeing. I was getting tired of being used as a punching bag and ending up in the Emergency Room for him to get pain pills. When my pain was unbearable, I would take a pain pill. However, he thought I was taking them to get high like he was. He would take five pills at a time and then several more about an hour later. Sometime it was even more than that. Again, my hidden pill bottle was getting filled. I was terrified of becoming addicted to the pills as he was and what would happen to me if he found the bottle. I knew in my heart we could not continue this way. Something needed to be done, but what was I to do?

Sometimes I compared myself to Jesus Christ. Jesus suffered for our sins and paid for them with his life. As I was being abused by Steven, it felt as though I was suffering for his sins. I used to pray all the time for God to set me free. What I didn't realize was that I didn't want to be set free. I didn't trust enough in my faith that Jesus would take care of me and I would be all right. There were many opportunities to get out and go to a shelter, but I stayed.

Chapter 5

Stabbed and Abandoned

Things had been going bad between us. Steven's moods were always changing and I never knew what mood he was in. I was unable to relax around him and communication was rough. We could not get into a rhythm of love and harmony.

One day I was vacuuming the carpet and he would not leave me alone. He kept stepping in front of the vacuum whichever way I tried to go. I stopped trying to clean as nothing was getting done. He began to start a fight with me over something stupid. I said, "Stop! Leave me alone." I told him I couldn't take it anymore! He obviously didn't like hearing that and became angry. He started yelling and threw the laundry that I had just folded across the room. Scared and trying to get away from him, I ran down the hall and into our bedroom. He caught and pinned me with my back against the wall. Trying to push him off of me, he pressed harder onto me. Suddenly, there was an excruciating pain in the lower left-hand side of my abdomen. He had just stabbed me with a pair of scissors. I couldn't believe that he had just stabbed me. Blood was going everywhere. I asked him to call an ambulance and he said "No!" I was pleading with him to get help for me. I thought he was going to leave me there to bleed to death! He then said that he would take me to a UMC Quick Care only if I told them that I tripped over the vacuum cord with the scissors in my hand. It made no sense to me, but I went along with it because I needed medical attention immediately.

When we arrived at UMC Quick Care, they took me into the back right away. The doctor quickly came in to see me and after looking at the wound stated that I needed to go to a hospital as it was a life threatening injury and they couldn't treat me there. They wanted to call an ambulance to take me, but Steven told them he would take me there instead. In the car, he told me that I better not tell them how my injury really happened or he would kill me.

We went straight to the Emergency Room at Sunrise Hospital and I was attended to right away. Steven stayed by my side to make sure that I didn't tell anyone what really happened. The doctor came in to treat my injury and asked how it happened. We told them the story he wanted me to say. The doctor looked at my wound and said he needed to get a Surgeon. The doctor said "If the scissors had pierced my abdomen, it would be fatal, as my bowel would enter my bloodstream". Steven was then told to go wait in the waiting room.

After he left the room, the Surgeon came in and looked at my wound and told me that he needed to cut me open wider so that he could see if the abdomen wall had been pierced. He then looked me straight in the eyes and asked me what really happened. He said "He did this to you, didn't he?" I said, "Yes". Then he asked me how and I told him that he would not leave me alone and he chased me into our bedroom, pinned me against the wall and stabbed me with the scissors.

They immediately prepped me right there in the Emergency Room to check my wound. They had no time to put me to sleep. They gave me a local anesthetic to numb the area. I didn't want them not to put me to sleep, as I was afraid I wouldn't wake up if they did. I could hear everything the Surgeon was saying. After a few moments he said, "I can't believe it, he just missed it." My wound was then stitched up and the Surgeon told me that I was very lucky and it was a miracle that my abdomen was not pierced. I said, "Jesus saved my life".

The Surgeon then told me that whenever a stab wound comes into the hospital, they have to inform the police. I begged him not to inform the police, as I was afraid of my husband. He told me that he had to and that he would make sure that I would be in good hands. He said, "This was attempted murder, he tried to kill you".

A Domestic Violence Counselor and two police officers came to take a report. They asked me what had happened and I began to cry. My eyes told the story; they knew I was a victim of domestic violence. I told them that I was afraid to tell them because the Devil was in the waiting room. They told me that they could not protect me unless I told them what really happened. The officers tried to get me to press charges against Steven for attempted murder and domestic violence. I told them I was not going to press charges against him because I was afraid of him. With no money and nowhere to go except a shelter, I didn't think they could help me. They told me that they would protect me and that there might not be a next time, as he would probably kill me. Still, I refused and begged them not to tell him that they knew what happened.

In the waiting room, the officers told him that I had told them that I fell over the cord and it was standard procedure for them to talk to him. The Domestic Violence Counselor had informed them that I had been there several times before for injuries that he inflicted on me. The officers told him that they believed that he stabbed me and tried to kill me. And they told him never to lay a hand on me again or he would be arrested. He was then allowed to come into my room to see me. The Surgeon told him he was lucky that I was still alive.

Upon returning home with Steven, I was convinced I was married to someone with serious mental issues. It felt like I was in a bad dream. He wanted me to get over it, but I couldn't. Being stabbed changed everything; my feelings for him became numb. I was no longer interested in fixing things our marriage. There was very little said between us. He continued to act like it never happened and he even tried to brainwash me into believing that I fell over the vacuum cord. And at one point he even tried to convince me that I stabbed myself.

Deep inside I really hated him and myself for not being strong enough to walk away. I was stupid for allowing him to get and maintain control of everything in my life. I would constantly pray to God for help. God put help right in front of me and I never saw it or didn't want to see it. This was not the happy ending I had always dreamed about.

I asked my mother to move in with us because I was afraid to be alone with him. He liked the idea of her moving in to help pay the mortgage. I wanted her there to protect me if he did anything to me. He kept saying that he would never hit me or hurt me again, but he had told me that before.

My mother moved in with us shortly thereafter. Steven and I were not talking much so it was comforting to have her there. I was still terrified of him and with her there I felt some safety. She knew we were having big problems, but she didn't know that he had stabbed me, as I didn't tell anyone. I felt like an idiot for not having him arrested. He would have gone to jail and never been able to hurt me again. I knew it would only be a matter of time before something happened again.

The next few months went by without any acts of violence, probably because my mother was there. It was nice having her there, she cooked us dinner and helped me keep the place clean as I had very little ambition to do anything for him. He was still taking pills and didn't seem to care much about me. Having my mother there was good for me, but he wanted her to move out. After three months of living with us, she moved out. It was sad for me to see her go. I wanted to go with her.

A few weeks passed since my mother moved out and my relationship with him was still bad. He continued trying to brainwash me into believing that I fell over the vacuum and stabbed myself and I think that he actually started believing it himself.

Just when I thought that things couldn't get any worse in my life, they did. It started out as a normal day, he was getting ready for work. He came up to me and gave me a kiss and said, "I love you". As usual, I watched him get into our car from our front door and he waived good-bye. I laid down to take a nap and wait for his call. He would always call me either when he arrived at work or on his first break. Suddenly, I woke up with a terrible feeling that something was not right. It was half way though his shift and he had not called me yet! I called him at work and couldn't get a hold of him, his co-workers were giving me the run-around. My gut feeling told me something was really wrong. He took the car, so I called a cab and went to see him at work. On the way there, my heart was pounding in my chest, I was terrified at what might be wrong!

When I arrived at The Golden Gate Casino in Downtown Las Vegas, I went inside to find him. His supervisor told me that he was not there and he took a leave of absence. I couldn't believe what I was hearing. Not knowing what to do, I began to cry. Everything in my life depended on him.

On the cab ride home, I was in shock and was asking myself why did he do this? The cab ride cost me almost everything I had. We lived in a small-gated community and we needed a key to enter. The key was in our car, so I had to wait outside for some one to enter for me to get in. It was about 9 p.m. so there was not much traffic. I sat on the curb and waited for quite a while and finally decided to climb over the wall to get in. As I was sliding over the top of the wall, my hand slipped and I fell to the ground cutting my knee on the sprinkler head.

Upon entering our condo, I called Steven's mother to find out if she knew what was going on. She told me that she had no idea, but I knew she was lying. The rest of the night seemed to last an eternity as I tried to figure out why he was doing this to me. He didn't show any sign of him leaving or even a letter explaining why. He took our only car and drained all of the money out of our accounts. I was abandoned with no money, no car and no job to support myself. The next day I called his father to see if he knew anything and he also said, "No". He asked me if I needed anything, but being too ashamed to ask for help, I told him I was all right.

Three long days went by and the phone finally rang. I answered it hoping it would be him, but it wasn't. It was his mother, she was calling to tell me that Steven was never coming back to Las Vegas and that our marriage was over. She told me to get rid of all his things. I asked her if I could speak to my husband and she said, "NO! He is not here". Then she hung up on me. I was devastated. Even after everything he had done to me, I loved him and thought we were supposed to be together. In my heart and mind, we were soul mates.

I began having an emotional breakdown and called my mother. She came and took me to the hospital where I willingly admitted myself. In the hospital they informed me that I was a victim of domestic violence and had post-traumatic stress syndrome. It was hard on my mother watching me have this breakdown, hurting her was the last thing I wanted to do.

While resting in the hospital, I continued to try to find Steven. Everyone tried to convince me to forget him and move on with my life, but needing to know why he left me consumed my every thought. I again called his mother and told her I was in the hospital and needed to talk to Steven. She still said that she didn't know where he was and for me to go on with my life. I informed her that he took our car and all of our money and left me with nothing, but she didn't care. After five days, I was released from the hospital and was told that I needed to go to counseling for domestic violence. Not knowing what to do, I asked my mother to move back in with me and she did

When I returned to our condo, I did just what his mother told me to, I threw all of his things in the trash. Not having money or food, I placed a classified add in the paper to sell his some of his other things. A man named Kenneth came by to buy his weight bench and felt sorry for me. He bought me some food and asked me if I wanted to go to church with him. It was like God had sent me an angel to help me through these hard times. We became friends and he helped me get back on my feet.

I called my oldest brother, Ronnie. We were not very close and told him what had happened to me. He shocked me when he offered to lend me some money to get a car, as he knew that without a car it would be hard to find a job. I accepted and bought an inexpensive car and filed for divorce.

Going to church helped me accept the fact that it was really over. However, I was depressed and had no energy or ambition to do much of anything. I was feeling sorry for myself and in a sick way, I was really missing him. The next few weeks were hard and I began to get angry. I would pray to God to please let Steven call so that I could tell him how much I hated him and slam down the phone. However, the phone never rang!

About two months after he left me, my divorce was close to being final. It felt like I was divorcing Steven's mother as all the paperwork went through her. I was still praying to God for the phone to ring. My relationship with God is what kept me going. In my heart, I believed there was a reason for everything even though I didn't understand it. My heart and soul were filled with faith that God would get me through this low point in my life.

The three years I spent with Steven broke me down. I was no longer the same vibrant girl who was confident and saw life as a movie as I went through it. Inside, I was dying, he was suffocating me and taking my identity away from me.

Kenneth became a close friend to me and he would take me to church every Sunday. He continued to bring me food and my favorite, Diet Dr. Pepper. My mother really liked him, which was a big difference from Steven. I believe that God brings angels into our lives to help us through hard times and I believe that Kenneth was my angel. I was very grateful for the kindness he brought into my life when I needed it most. I told him that we could only be friends and made it as clear as I could from the beginning.

When I went to counseling, the therapist told me that I would go through men like wild fire. This assumption made me mad, because I knew it wouldn't happen as my heart still belonged to Steven. Most of my days were spent laying around and wishing we were together. I didn't understand how he could just forget about me. My twenty-seventh birthday came and went. I received cards and flowers from people, but nothing from Steven. That hurt me deeply.

In early September a friend of mine came over to lay out at the pool with me. While at the pool I went to get the mail. When I looked at the mail I froze, it was a letter from Steven. The letter was short, it only said, "I am with my mother and grandmother and if I needed anything that is where I could reach him". That's all it said. Immediately, I became irate and ripped it into as many pieces as I could and threw it away. Then my day continued normally, that was conformation to me that I was doing the right thing.

Time seemed to lag on forever, but was really going by rather quickly. It was October 3, 1990, the day before my divorce would be final. At this point I was convinced that it was over and I was dealing with it, excepting the fact that my call was never going to come and I would never get the chance to hang up on him. At 4 a.m. the phone rang and I answered it. I said, "Hello". The man on the other end said, "Hi, Tami". I didn't recognize the man's voice and I asked, "Who is this?" The voice said, "This is your husband!"

Chapter 6

Back Together

Laying there with the phone in my hand, frozen and in disbelief I asked, "Who?" The voice on the other end of the line responded, "It's Steven".

I thought to myself, oh my God! My prayers had been answered! Now was my chance to tell him how much he had hurt me by walking out on me, and then hang up the phone, but I couldn't. I was in a state of disbelief that I really had him on the phone. I had waited for this moment and rehearsed what I would say when he called. Now here was my chance and I was unable to say anything I had rehearsed. By me not hanging up the phone, it felt like I had failed the Lord and myself.

I asked him, "Why are you calling me now, after all this time?"

He replied, "I'm still your husband and I love you!" Then he stated, "I thought you would have changed the phone number by now."

Hearing him say that lit a spark in me and I quickly became angry for what he had done to me, irritated I responded, "You left me with nothing, not a word, no note, nothing! How can you say that you love me?"

Calmly, he began to explain to me that his mother had a lot to do with him leaving and staying away.

I explained to him that our divorce would be final at 5 p.m. the next day.

He said, "I don't want a divorce. I still wear my wedding ring and I never took it off. I wanted to come back to you, but my mother kept persuading me not to."

I asked, "How long are you going to allow your mother to tell you what to do? She wanted to split us up since we met"

"If you take me back, I will not let her interfere with our lives again," he quietly stated. "I never stopped loving you and I should not have left you." He continued on by saying, "After I left, I became suicidal. I went up a mountain and wanted to jump off. My life without you seemed hopeless"

As I heard him say that, a flood of emotions came over me that I had been trying to bury since he left. My heart was pounding in my chest like a sledgehammer and I realized what I had already known, I still loved him very much!

He told me that he was no longer taking pain pills, but he had started smoking again. Thinking to myself, I can deal with that as long as we are together!

I asked him, "Where are you now?"

He said, "I left my mother's place and moved to Reno, Nevada."

As he began to tell me about what he was doing now, all I could think about was being with him again. He told me how nice it was in Reno, playing on the things that I enjoy the most. He said, "There's beautiful scenery everywhere with trees, open land and mountains. It even snows here in the winter."

I began to picture how beautiful it must be there. Then he continued on by telling me about his job, he started working in a casino as a slot tech in one of the casino's. It was more enjoyable to him because it was a calmer lifestyle up there as compared to Las Vegas. The friends he made at his job were telling him that just because you break up, doesn't mean it has to be forever! That is why he decided to call me and talk.

He said to me, "I don't want to get a divorce, you are my wife and I will do whatever it takes to fix this mess I created in our marriage."

Although my feelings for him were rushing back to the surface, I didn't tell him I would take him back. He asked if he could see me. Knowing that seeing him in person would be a mistake as I was finally getting back on my feet, I agreed. We continued to talk for a few hours, which seemed to fly by. The entire time talking to him, I was still in shock. I was convinced that I would never hear from him again and couldn't believe it was happening. It had been just over three months since he had deserted me and caused me tremendous pain, however, I was looking forward to seeing him.

He immediately made airline reservations to come to Las Vegas, he arrived just after noon on October 4. I was waiting at the gate with butterflies in my stomach, as I didn't know what to expect. The anticipation of seeing him was killing me. Suddenly, there he was walking towards me. I was taken back by his appearance. He had gained quite a few pounds and his hair was long and scraggly. It was not appealing to me seeing him like that. I was wondering if he would like what he saw as well. Since he left me, I had lost some weight from the stress he threw upon me.

He looked at me and said, "Oh my God, you are so beautiful!"

Then he asked me if he could give me a hug. I reached out with my arms towards him and we hugged each other. We held on as tight as we could for what seemed to be an eternity. What a wonderful feeling it was to be in his arms again, it felt just like it did when we first fell in love with each other.

We were holding hands as we walked out of the airport and to my car. When we arrived at my car, I informed him that it was my car and I will be driving! We decided to go out by the lake and get something to eat and talk. He told me that he didn't know what he was doing when he left me and his mother was strongly influencing him to leave. We both knew that she didn't want us to be together from the beginning. She never liked me and didn't want to get to know me. As we sat there talking for several hours, I made a decision. I don't know if I wanted to be with him or needed to be with him. But, I thought my place was with him. We decided to give our marriage another try. I called my divorce attorney and cancelled the divorce. He was still my husband! He looked at my left hand and noticed that my wedding ring was not there. He asked me, "Where is your wedding ring?"

I replied, "After you left me with no money, I had to sell it to get by."

"You need to buy a new one then," he stated. This hurt me a little as I felt that he should buy me a new ring to show his love for me. "Until you can buy a real one, you need to get a fake one so people will know that you are married!" he continued.

Not wanting my mother to know we were back together, we went to the Gold Coast Hotel & Casino and checked into a suite. The next few days we stayed there getting comfortable with each other as I needed to know if I really wanted to be with him again. As always in the past he would be a perfect gentleman to get me to relax and fall under his control. My mother didn't know that I was with him, she thought I went out of town with friends. When I called to tell her the truth, she was furious! She told me I was stupid and making a big mistake! When we went back to our condo, my mother seemed to be ok with us getting back together. She said, "If you love him, be with him."

Not wanting to move back to Las Vegas, he told me that he really liked living in Reno. He began courting me about how nice it was there, how much cooler the weather was and telling me about some of the places he would take me to gaze upon beautiful scenery. He also told me how much he enjoyed his job and the people he worked with. With me never really liking Las Vegas, it wasn't hard for him to convince me to leave. Still, not being sure I was making the right move, I suggested we go to counseling. "We don't need counseling," he told me, "we will be fine as long as we were together!" and that "I was his life." I wondered to myself, how could I be his life the way he had treated and abandoned me! But, I loved him and wanted a new start with him.

I flew back with him to see what it would be like living in Reno and with him again. It was mid-October, my favorite time of the year, there were pumpkins everywhere. The air was cool and brisk. Even to this day,

I can remember how the cold air felt on my face as we stepped out of the airport. We spent two wonderful weeks together, my love for him was growing as he was regaining control of me again. He now seemed to be the man of my dreams, a perfect gentleman, loving and caring. However, there was one problem. He didn't tell his mother exactly where he was or that we were back together. This was a problem because she was very possessive of him and never treated him like a grown man. She didn't respect him as a man or me as his wife. It seemed like the phone never stopped ringing as she constantly called him. He was determined not to talk to her, as she had a way of manipulating him into doing what she wanted him too.

Being with him again made me happy, as he was being a loving husband. I felt comforted by him taking care of me again and I didn't realize that he was regaining total control over me. He convinced me to move there with him permanently. I agreed and we found an apartment that was perfect for the two of us; it was a small two bedroom with a fireplace. It over looked a pasture that had cows roaming and there were mountains in the distance. I went back to Las Vegas to pack for the move and he flew back the next weekend.

Preparing my move to Reno to be with him was both exciting and scary. Exciting, because it felt like we were supposed to be together and he made me feel safe and secure. It was a fresh start for us both in a new place. It was scary, because I remembered how mean and violent he could be when he would snap and go into a fit of anger. Being back with each other for this short time he didn't show any sign of doing that again. I hoped it might have been the pills that made him act like that. I thought to myself that only time would tell!

We stayed at the Excalibur Hotel & Casino for a few days. I was caught up in the excitement of getting our new lives set up that I didn't realize my period was two weeks late! Realizing it didn't come I became frantic. Steven asked me, "What's wrong?" When I told him, he said, "Relax, if your pregnant, it's a gift from God and I will be the happiest man in the world!"

Needing to know if we were pregnant, we went out and bought a pregnancy test. It was positive! We were going to have a baby. Feeling stunned, shocked and scared, I began to think, what if he leaves me again, or what if he hurts me physically, or even worse, what if he abuses our child! Realizing my options were limited, I decided to go with it and be happy. I always wanted a child and thought I would be a great mother. Plus, with a child, he might actually continue to be this wonderful man.

We finished packing the U-haul and loaded my car onto a trailer. It was very hard to say, "Good-bye" to my mother. Never had I lived so far away from her. We both cried, it was a sad moment, but a new life was waiting for me in Reno. She wanted to stay in our condo in Las Vegas. As she was paying the mortgage we had no problem with that and we always had a place to go if we ever decided to move back.

It was a long ten-hour drive to Reno as there is nothing to look at. It was just open desert with Joshua trees and very little signs of human life. The road and a small building were about all we saw. We arrived around dusk and it was snowing lightly. I remember how beautiful and peaceful it was. It felt like angels were welcoming me to my new home as a tranquil feeling came over me.

It was fun for me to get the apartment set up as our home. I felt whole again because I had my other half by my side. It all seemed to good to be true and I worried that he might slip back into that monster he had been. I just hoped for the best!

We began to prepare for the baby; we started buying baby bottles, little diapers, and baby toys. It was so exciting. Steven began to work two jobs, because the cost of living in Reno was expensive compared to Las Vegas. And we needed things for the baby and had doctors to see.

One night while he was at work, I moved a chair and began to get a pain in my belly button. Worried, I called him at work and he said, "Relax and lay down, I will be home soon." The next day, we called the doctor and they told us it was normal and not to worry. Our appointment was a week away and the pain was deep and sharp. Not wanting to hurt the baby, I spent the next few days laying down as much as possible.

Four days into my bed rest, I went to the bathroom and there was blood, a lot of blood. Panicking, I started to cry out, "Oh no! Please God no!" Steven heard me and came to the bathroom and opened the door. He saw the blood and I could see his eyes begin to tear up. We went to the Emergency Room and thought for sure that we were having a miscarriage. They did an ultra-sound and we could see the heart beating. The doctor said, "Everything is fine, Mom and Dad. The baby's strong and it's fine." We were so relieved. Hugging each other tightly I could feel our souls merging, oh what a wonderful feeling it was.

When we went home, he was very strict. He told me that I was not to do anything at all except rest. So, that is exactly what I did. I enjoyed lying around watching television and having him take care of me and do all of the cleaning and cooking.

It was November 15, two weeks into my bed rest I started getting cramps. They came on fast and hard and the pain was barely tolerable. As I lay there, becoming more and more worried by the minute, I called to him in the other room, to let him know what was happening. He was worried and asked me what we should do. Not knowing myself, I suggested that I just lie there and rest. I continued to lay in bed for the next few hours with no relief. When I went to the bathroom, there was a lot of blood in the toilet. Scared, I cried out for him to come to help me. As he ran into the bathroom, he could see that I was crying. As I looked at him, he knew that it was bad and I could see him beginning to cry.

It was snowing heavily as he rushed me to the hospital. When we finally arrived at the hospital, which took a lot longer than it should have because of the snow, we were immediately taken into an examination room. As we were being examined, he stood by my side holding my hand. It was comforting for me to have him there as I felt something was really wrong with the baby and didn't want to be alone. The doctor and nurses were asking me a lot of questions and I could barely keep my composure as I answered them. Finally, the doctor looked at me and told us, "You are fully dilated and having a miscarriage." It was like my entire world was crashing down on me. I became hysterical and was begging the doctor to save my baby. He put his hand on my shoulder and said, "I'm sorry, there is nothing we can do for your baby."

Because I just lost the baby and was still bleeding, they admitted me. They found a room to put me in to rest and sedated me, however, I couldn't sleep. Steven told me that he was going to leave, as he had to go to work. Shocked and unable to believe that he was going to leave me alone just after we lost our baby, I felt betrayed and became very angry with him. Telling him, "No way are you leaving me here", he quickly decided better of that decision and spent the night with me in the hospital.

The next morning I was taken in for surgery to stop the bleeding. They performed a DNC. It was very traumatic for me when they returned me to my room. Since it was on the maternity floor, all around me were women with their babies and mine was gone. The nurses tried to tell me everything happens for a reason and there must have been something wrong with the baby. They tried to make me feel better, but it didn't help. The next morning, I was discharged and the doctors had given me a prescription for pain pills. I took them when I needed them and put the rest away.

Thanksgiving arrived and I didn't feel like I had anything to give thanks for. I was unbelievably sad and still cried everyday. I didn't want to cook a Thanksgiving dinner, but he persuaded me to cook. He might have thought it would be good for me to cook and get my mind off the baby. I didn't enjoy cooking the dinner, as usually I loved cooking. To make things worse, while eating dinner, my tooth broke and instantly began causing me pain. After we ate dinner, I took a pain pill to help with the pain. He wanted to take some pills to get high. At this point, I was so depressed that I didn't care anymore and let him take my pills. If I had said, "No!" he would have probably taken them anyway.

The next day, he took me to the dentist. As usual, the dentist gave me pain pills and antibiotics. He informed me that in addition to my broken tooth, my wisdom teeth needed to be removed as they were impacted.

After losing the baby, Steven changed and didn't seem to want to be around me, I think he was hurting in his own way and didn't want to talk to me about it. He turned back to the pills instead of coming to me. I never dreamt that the nightmare would start all over again, but it was.

With losing the baby and him becoming distant from me, I no longer wanted to stay in Reno. I felt trapped and alone and I needed someone to be there for me and I knew it would not be him. I talked to him about my desire to move back to Las Vegas. Surprisingly, he agreed and we began to make plans to move back.

Losing our baby ten days before Thanksgiving was difficult enough. It felt like we had very little to give thanks for. Instead of the Christmas spirit in December, it was sorrow and tears. There was no Christmas spirit in either of us. I felt dead inside.

We informed my mother of our plans to come back to Las Vegas. She was happy that I was all right and coming home. She was still living in our condo and needed to find a new place to stay. She quickly found an apartment a few minutes from our condo so that she would still be close to me. Steven didn't want to move back into our condo because of all the bad things that happened there. However, we had little choice, as we needed a place to stay. We decided to move back into our condo until we could find a new place to live. It was mid January when we were ready to move. I didn't want to drive back, so when we were ready to move, I flew back to Las Vegas. Desert Storm had just broken out and I had to deal with extra security at the airport. Steven packed our things and drove back by himself.

I was expecting him back at our condo and was looking forward to seeing him. I was worn out, as I had gone through so much in a short time, moving to Reno, getting pregnant, losing the baby and moving back to Las Vegas. I was hoping for a quiet night at home with my husband to help me get my spirit up.

When he finally arrived, I knew that he would be tired, so I had a simple meal and cold drink waiting for him. As he walked in, I could tell something was not right. He had the look of the devil on his face and I thought to myself, oh no, not again! This was the first time he had been in the condo since he left me months before. We were in the living room and I asked him, "What is wrong? Are you all right?"

He responded in a cold tone, "Nothing. Just leave me alone."

Scared, I slowly turned away and went to the bedroom. He had not shown me any of this behavior since we had been back together and it felt like here we go again. I began wondering if I should try to help him adjust to being back in Las Vegas or leave and stay with my mother. Since I loved him, I quickly decided to stay with him. I figured he might have just had a rough trip back and he had to do it by himself, which probably was not easy or much fun.

A few days slowly passed and he was still agitated. I calmly asked him, "What's wrong?"

He responded, "I don't like living here. There are too many bad memories in this place."

We were behind on the payments, as I could not pay the mortgage after he left me high and dry and we could not catch up. I tried to make him feel better and told him, "Let's sell it and find a new place to live." He liked that idea and we began looking into selling the condo. He began working at Whiskey Pete's Hotel & Casino in Primm, Nevada, which is about a 40-minute drive outside of Las Vegas.

We found an ad in the paper stating: WE BUY HOUSES! We called and began the process. We had been in the condo about three months when we believed that we had sold it. Thinking that we sold the condo, we moved in with my mother, she had a one-bedroom apartment and we stayed on the floor in the dining room. It turned out that we had been conned out of the condo. The people we thought bought the condo rented it out. In reality, we never sold it and it was foreclosed on us. It was a very stressful and confusing time for the both of us.

We lived on the floor at my mother's for about nine months. Things between Steven and myself were tense at times and good at others. Until one day around Halloween, while my mother was at work, he clicked. He began having another fit of anger. It caught me of guard as things were going pretty good between us. He started yelling at me and called me a "Fucking Bitch!" I was scared and upset and I began to turn away from him. Suddenly, he grabbed my arm and threw me to the ground like I was a rag doll. He came down on top of me, pinning me to the ground with his body. He quickly wrapped his hands around my neck and began to squeeze, his grip was so tight it felt like a rope was strangling me. Unable to breath, I thought this is it. I was going to die! I tried to fight him off of me, but it was useless. I began begging him with my eyes to please stop and let me go. As I began to lose consciousness, he released his grip on my neck and got up off of me and began walking away. As he left, he knocked the table over and threw the chairs against the walls. He turned to look at me after his rampage, I thought he was going to come after me again as he had the look of the devil on his face, but he walked out of the apartment and left in the car.

After I caught my breath and composed myself a bit, I went to the bathroom to look at my neck. I could see the red imprint of both of his hands around my neck. I just stared at myself in the mirror and began to cry. Wondering to myself, who is this girl in the mirror? How could I be so weak and stupid to let someone abuse me like this? I cried for hours and then I heard the door opening. I was hoping it was my mother because I was still terrified of him and what he might do to me when he returned, but to my horror, it was him. He came in and sat down on the couch like nothing ever happened. He didn't say anything to me and I didn't say a word to him because he might go off on me again. So I just sat there quietly in the corner of the dining room, trying not to make a noise.

When my mother came home, I never told her what he had done to me because I didn't think there was anything she could do for me. That was a big mistake on my part. She could have and would have kicked him out and she probably would have had him arrested. But she never knew!

Things between Steven and myself were extremely tense for the next month or so. Just after the New Year, 1993, he told me he was tired of living on the floor and he wanted to get a place of our own. We were pretty stable financially, so I agreed. We ended up getting our own apartment in the same complex as my mother. This scared me, being alone with him again, but with my mother's apartment just around the corner, I thought it would be all right. At least if I needed her, I would have been able to walk!

Several months went by and things were going good between us. Well, he had not had a fit of anger in a while. He was taking the pills everyday and I was his way of getting them, it was doctor after doctor. He didn't care about the pain I was in as long as he kept getting his fix.

I was getting bored sitting around waiting for him to get home from work everyday. Not wanting to be left with nothing again and wanting to better myself, I began thinking of a career that I would enjoy and be able to support myself with if he ever left me again. I thought long and hard and decided to get into doing nails, manicures and pedicures. I told him that I wanted to go to Cosmetology school. He said, "That's fine with me." In May 1993, I enrolled at Rollers School of Cosmetology. At first, it was hard for me to attend school full-time with all the stress and fear at home, but after a few weeks it became a release for me. I loved getting out and doing something I enjoyed and it also helped me to regain a little confidence in myself.

Chapter 7
My Rights Violated

On June 5, 1993, I didn't feel good, so I stayed home from school. Steven went to work and told me to call him if I needed anything. Shortly after he left, my mother brought lunch to me, chicken noodle soup. After I finished eating, I wanted to lie down so my mother left. Just after I laid down the phone rang. It was Steven calling from work to see how I was doing which made me feel happy.

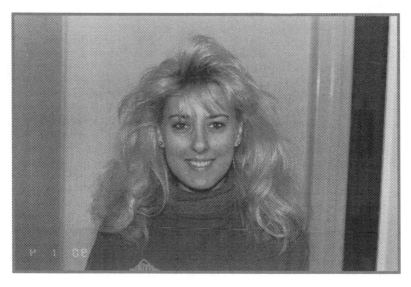

This is a picture of me about this time.

About 1 p.m., while lying down watching TV, I was about to fall asleep when all of the sudden I heard loud noises outside, they were quickly getting louder and louder. The sound was coming from the stairs outside my door. It sounded like people running up the stairs and pounding their feet on each step as hard as they could. I was scared and confused as it was normally a quiet place. The noise was loud and I just froze, listening and wondering what was going on out there. Then my heart stopped as they began to pound on my door.

They yelled, "Police, open up or we are coming in"

Startled, I quickly sat up in bed and said, "Oh my God!" I was naked and didn't know what to do. I yelled back to them, "Just a minute, just a minute. I don't have any clothes on."

He responded, "You have 30 seconds or this door is coming off!"

I ran to the ironing board and grabbed a tee shirt and began to pull it over my head as I heard him say, "Times up this door is coming down."

As I turned the door handle, they pushed their way in. The door knocked me back a few feet by the force of their push. There were three men, two police officers and the maintenance man from the complex. Looking at them, I said, "What's wrong? Why are you in my house?"

One of the police officers said, "Don't move. Stay right where you are."

The maintenance man said, "You didn't pay your rent. You are being evicted!"

Then, the police officers said, "I'm going to have to lock you out of the apartment."

At this point, I was scared to death and began to cry. They didn't come and knock on the door gently and calmly. This event came on like an attack. I didn't know what to do. I cried to them, "What do you mean? We paid our rent! You're making a mistake, you have the wrong person."

The maintenance man said, "Well, I don't think so."

The police officer quickly jumped in and said, "We would not be here if you paid your rent!" I quickly began to think this couldn't be happening, Steven did it to me again!

The maintenance man then said, "You should have paid your rent, Miss."

Then it dawned on me that I was standing in front of these three men that I had never seen before with nothing on but a tee shirt. I asked them, "Can I get dressed?"

The police officer glared at me slowly from top to bottom with a dirty smirk on his face and said, "No, Just stay right there." He stood there glaring at me with piercing eyes; it felt like he was violating me with his eyes. Here I stood in front of these three strange men in my home half naked, I had never been so humiliated in my life.

Then the maintenance man looked at the officers and said, "I guess I'll leave now." He then turned and walked out, followed by the other police officer. Now, there was just one policeman in the apartment with me.

"Can I please get my clothes on now?" I asked again. I thought to myself, why can't I get dressed? I felt naked standing there in front of him with only a tee shirt on. Scared, I said, "You have made a mistake, you're in the wrong apartment. We paid our rent."

He responded, "I don't make mistakes, I would not be here if you paid your rent."

I told him, "I can get you the receipt and show you that we paid the rent."

He exclaimed to me, "I do not make mistakes. I'm going to lock up your belongings in the apartment and you will be locked off the property."

Now I was terrified and crying. I said, "I have to get some clothes on." I slowly began to turn towards the bedroom.

He yelled, "Stop! Don't move stay right there!"

Startled, I said, "Please, don't lock me out, we paid our rent. I have the receipt."

He said, "Then why are you so upset? If you would have paid your rent, this would not be happening to you and I would not be here."

Still crying, I begged him again, "Please, let me get dressed."

In an angry voice he said, "You're not moving!"

I asked him, "Can I please talk to him?"

He said, "No." Then he spoke into the phone, "If she pays the rent and fees, can she stay in the apartment?" The owner said, "Yes." The police officer looked at me and shook his head, yes. I was so glad that this nightmare was almost over. He continued talking into the phone, "I'm placing her in custody and bringing her to the office."

When he hung up the phone, I asked, "Can I get dressed now?"

Finally, he said, "Yes."

He followed me down the hall and into my bedroom. It was very uncomfortable for me to have this stranger in my bedroom even though he was a police officer. I asked him, "Can I have some privacy?"

He said, "No."

He stood just inside the doorway of my bedroom as I put on some sweatpants. With the stress and horror I was going through, he saw more than he should have of my body but what choice did I have? Now that I was dressed, he began walking me to the office. The embarrassment he had done to me was bad enough, but walking out of the apartment, several of my neighbors were standing there starring at me. I felt so humiliated by the events of this day and it just kept getting worse. We went down the stairs and walked a few yards when I realized that I had forgotten the rental receipts. I looked at him and said, "I forgot my money!"

He shook his head in aggravation and said, "Do you even have the money to pay your rent?"

I responded, "Yes!"

Then with his right arm, he directed me back towards the apartment and said, "After you." We turned back and headed up the stairs. When we arrived at the apartment, he let me go inside alone as he waited outside. I quickly went to the bedroom to get the receipt and grabbed the phone and called Steven at work. I was hysterical, he could not understand anything I was saying at first. He said, "Calm down, what's wrong?"

I told him, "I have to hurry, the police are here and the apartment people say that we have to move because we didn't pay our rent. We are being evicted!"

In a very stern voice he said, "That's bullshit!"

I was crying and begged him, "Please, help me!"

He said, "Try to calm down. I will call the office and find out what's going on." Having him know what I was going through made me feel a little better. It felt like I was no longer alone, my husband was going to help me. I hung up the phone, still very upset and went back outside. I told the police officer, "I have it. Let's go."

When we walked into the office, the owner looked at me as I stood there crying and said, "Oh, Oh, Come in here and sit down. I am on the phone with Stephen. Everything's going to be ok."

He handed me the phone and I heard Steven say, "It's ok. I know what happened, it has been taken care of. Now go home and call me when you get there."

I was happy it was finally over. I hung up the phone and the owner told the police officer, "You went to the wrong apartment." The police officer said something to the owner that I couldn't hear and walked away. He didn't tell me he was sorry, he just walked away.

I just sat there for a few moments to compose myself. The owner said, "I'm so sorry you had to go through this." I looked at him and didn't know what to say, it was very traumatizing to me. I went back to my apartment by myself to make sure he was not there. After I checked my apartment, I decided to go and stay at my mother's apartment until Steven came home from work.

As I walked down the stairs, I saw the officer at another apartment on the first floor. He was banging on the door, ordering them to open up, just as he had done to me. He looked at me and said, "You better take this as a warning, your name was on the list and you better consider yourself lucky!"

I didn't say anything to him and went to my mother's apartment. When she opened the door, she looked at me and said, "Oh my God!

What's wrong?" She brought me inside and sat me down. I told her about my ordeal and just cried and cried until Steven came home.

This event changed me. I no longer felt safe in my apartment. Whenever I was alone, it always felt like they were going to bust in on me again. My health was affected by the stress of this event also, immediately after this happened, I began to break out in hives. The hives started as red itchy patches all over my body and quickly went into my lips swelling up making my face look very distorted. After seeing several doctors and having many tests done, it was determined and diagnosed that the hives were caused by stress. The tests showed that I was not allergic to anything. My body, mind and spirit had been through so much by the abuse in my life that it could take no more and began to breakdown. I was put on steroids to control the hives; this caused me to gain weight. I also needed to carry an Epi-Pen with me at all times in case of a severe hive attack.

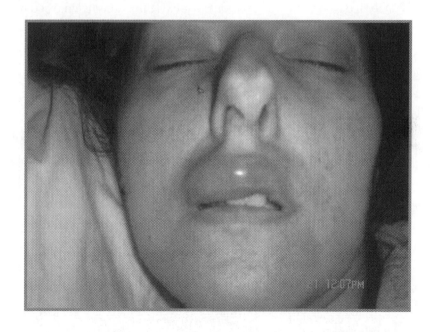

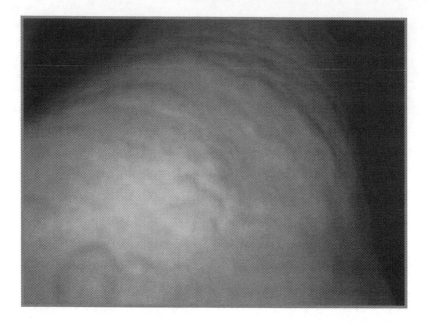

He had to pay for what he had done to me. He mistakenly charged into my apartment and terrified me and raped me with his eyes for just over an hour and never showed any remorse for what he did to me. This incident was reported on the local news broadcast and was in the newspaper. We contacted a lawyer and began a lawsuit. My attorney ordered us not to talk to the media as it could hurt the case.

The day I had been waiting for finally arrived, the day of my deposition. I didn't set out to destroy anybody, but I needed to have justice served and to make sure this didn't happen to anyone else. The police officer's name was Dick Drake. He was actually a Constable. He was denying everything that happened that day. I told the truth and prayed that the truth would come out.

I was very stressed about seeing the man that shattered my feeling of safety in my own home. The days leading up to the deposition, I had bad hive attacks. I was very traumatized, even though my attorney and husband were with me.

Waiting in the hallway, my heart stopped and there was a lump in my throat when I saw him walking up with his representation. Unable to say anything to him, I just stared at him. He never looked at me.

When we were called into the room and sat down at the table, there was a smell of alcohol coming from him. I never once took my eyes off of him. I wanted him to look me in the eyes and try to lie and say he didn't do anything. I prayed hard that somehow the truth would be told. He was a police officer and he had already lied about what happened that day. However, I knew the truth and had faith he would tell the truth. I continued to stare into his eyes and finally our eyes met. I stared deep into his eyes and into his soul and demanded him to tell the truth with my eyes.

I was shocked when out of nowhere, he broke down and admitted everything that he had done that day. He told the truth and validated my allegations. It felt like a huge weight had been lifted off of me. I thanked God for helping me get some closure. Unfortunately, by him admitting everything didn't take away the damage that he had already done to me. This horrible event left me with Post-Traumatic Stress Syndrome. Any loud noise would make me jump and I now had a hard time sleeping at night. Every noise I heard outside of my apartment startled me. I no longer felt safe when I was home alone.

A short time after this, Steven and I were walking through the Gold Coast casino and we saw him. He lost his job as a Constable and was now working there as a security guard. I felt sorry for him. What he did to me affected his life as well. Even though he was responsible for the attack on me, it was sad to see him like that. I am not a vindictive person and have forgiven him and wish him well with his life.

Chapter 8
Feeling Like A Machine

The next six months went by with me having continuous outbreaks of the hives. I had to stop going to Cosmetology School because of the hives, which made me very sad and I felt confined to my home. When I would have an outbreak, I would get red itchy patches all over my body and my lips would swell up like a balloon. Steven was not supportive to me. If he truly loved me, he would've been compassionate towards my condition and me. Unfortunately, he wasn't and would say many mean things to me. He would call me deformed and laugh at me. He was not helpful and the extra stress he put on me made the hives worse.

One day we went to eat at the Café at the Texas Station Casino. While there, I broke out in the hives and my lips swelled. Whenever the hives made my face swell, I knew I looked terrible and didn't want anyone to see me, not even my husband. He was embarrassed to be with me and to make things worse, a young boy eating with his family saw me and started to laugh at me. I wanted to cry, he wouldn't even walk out of the café with me. After that, he wouldn't take me anywhere. He made me stay at home. He told me, "You're hideous. You need to stay in the house where nobody can see you when you are like this." My self-esteem plummeted and I became depressed. I began to just hide from the world. It was a very hard time for me. With the hives, my spirit was broken and I felt deformed and plagued. The one person that should have been there for me turned out to be my worst enemy.

Look At Me

Look at me, laugh at me
Think what you want
Look at me and you will be blown away
I'm the wind, I'm the rain and I'm the sunshine
Full of rainbows, sugar and spice and moon beams too
Look someone in the eye before you judge them
Who knows they might become a great friend
Look at me and laugh
I'll be laughing till the end
Look above
Look up and thank Jesus the Christ
That you're alive
Look at me don't dare laugh
The God in me might just want to make you strive
Look me in the eye
You just might see a friend
What a surprise
Look at me and we'll join hands and look up above
And thank God that we're alive
Look anyone in the eye
And you might see
That they've suffered unbearable pain
They stood in the rain all alone
Because they had no place to call a home
Stand in their honor
I stand strong
I stand hand in hand
Brothers and sisters
We all bleed red blood
Be kind
Keep the strive
Stop laughing
Look inside and you
Might begin to cry!

During this time, he was lying to me about everything. I could smell the smoke on his breath and his clothes and yet he denied smoking. I always said, "Just tell me the truth and we can get through it."

He told me, "I work in a casino, people smoke there and it gets all over me."

I said, "I understand that, but it would not get on your breath that way." When I said that, he didn't know what to say and just shrugged his shoulders and turned and walked away from me.

He was caught speeding and was issued a traffic ticket and never told me about it. When I received a summons for him in the mail and asked him about it, he told me, I will take care of it." A few days later, I asked about it and he said, "I took care of it. It's paid." That was a lie it wasn't paid.

When we got back together, he stopped talking to his mother as she was constantly trying to get him to leave me. She was very possessive of him and didn't like that he would not talk to her. I later found out from one of his work friends that she went to see him at work. He was still working at Whiskey Pete's Casino in Stateline, NV at this time and he didn't want to see her. She refused to leave without talking to him and held some employees in the employee cafeteria. He still refused and she was arrested and 86'd from the casino. When you get 86'd from a casino that means that you will be arrested for trespassing if you ever return. It was something that he should have told me, it was not his fault that she went there.

I wonder how many other things he lied to me about that I didn't know about. When he would have a fit of anger and go away for several days, I always wondered if he was having an affair. To this day I don't know for sure, but I kept wondering.

It was his day off from work and we had just finished eating lunch. He stood up from the table and began mumbling something that I couldn't make out.

I asked, "What did you say?" in an average tone. I thought we had a good vibe going, so my tone was not aggressive or mean, I just didn't understand what he said.

He snapped and started yelling and calling me horrible names. I was stunned and wondered what had happened to him. Everything between us was going good and all of the sudden he changed back into a monster. He grabbed his plate and threw it against the wall. The plate broke into several pieces fell to the floor. Then he began to tear the place apart, knocking everything off the kitchen counter and making a mess of the place.

I started to cry and begged him, "Please, stop!"

He glared at me and responded, "Shut the fuck up!" When I heard that, I immediately stood up and went towards the bedroom for safety. Just before I entered the bedroom, I heard him say in a calmer voice, "Tami." I stopped in the doorway to the bedroom and turned towards him. He had grabbed the ironing board that was standing right there and shoved it into my abdomen like a knife several times. This pushed me into the bedroom and he followed. In pain, shocked and terrified I just stood there as his tirade continued, he threw the dresser over and everything on top of it crashed to the floor and scattered everywhere.

He pinned up against the wall with his right hand and punched me in the right side of my head with his left fist. The right side of my brain has scar tissue from an earlier car accident. That accident fractured my skull and my brain hemorrhaged into a blood clot, which killed a part of my brain. The worst thing for me was to be taking blows to my head. Then he took his hand off of me and walked away. I slid down the wall crying and in pain, stunned by what had just happened. He went out to the couch and sat down and fell asleep. After the pain in my head subsided, I went out to clean up the mess he had made. I worked as quietly as possible to not wake him up, fearing what could happen if he woke up. After I finished cleaning up the mess, I went to the bedroom and cried myself to sleep.

The next day, he woke up and went to work like nothing ever happened. He never apologized to me or made any mention of it ever happening. To this day, I don't know what set him off.

The next few months went by pretty smoothly, basically he did his thing and I did my own thing. I went back to finish school. It didn't take long for me to graduate because I was almost finished when I had to stop. Not wanting to be in the apartment anymore than I had to, I immediately started looking for a job. I started working at a little nail shop called The Nail Shack. It wasn't a great job, but it got me out of the house and back into the real world. Now, I had other people to talk to other than Steven. I was still too afraid to tell anyone about my personal life because I was terrified of my husband. Nobody should ever be afraid of their spouse, marriage is supposed to be a loving environment.

One of Steven's friends offered to rent his house to us. We both wanted to get out of the apartment and get into a new place. For me, the apartment didn't feel like a safe place. The memory of my attack was constantly in my thoughts. Even with my mother around the corner, I couldn't get comfortable when I was there alone. We moved into the house and again, it felt like we were getting a new start.

Steven was excited about me working so that he had more money to spend. Yes, when I came home from work, he was there waiting for me to give him the money I had just made. He would tell me that the money was being saved to buy a house of our own. I hated that he took my money and decided to hold a little back and hide it away for myself. He used some of it to buy a male Rottweiler puppy he named Clyde. I never had a dog before and really enjoyed having him around. In the picture, I'm laying with Clyde. A short time later, he wanted to breed the dog, so we bought two sister rottweilers. I named one Bon Bon and he named the other Snoopy.

With me working and us having the dogs around, he was being much nicer to me. There was no physical hostility towards the dogs or me. There was verbal abuse, but I just kept my mouth closed and it usually passed by without incident. However, he was still using me to get him pills, but it seemed to be a small price for me to pay as I felt I had the life I deserved. When we had puppies, it was a lot of fun and hard work taking care of them. I hated letting them go when we sold them, but the money was good.

Then one day Steven told me that he found a place that helped people in pain like me. I was pretty beat up at this point, my cracked skull, which gave me headaches on a regular basis, the herniated disc's in my back that he ruptured and now the hives. He told me, "We go to the clinic and drink a small cup of medicine and it takes away our pain."

I told him, "It sounds crazy!"

"You have to do it with me," he informed me. The clinic was in a run down and in a bad part of town. I didn't want to do it, but was afraid of the consequences if I didn't do it with him. It just didn't seem right to me, but he was in control. They interviewed us and asked a lot of questions that I was afraid to answer. They gave me a small cup to drink with a dull red liquid in it. It relieved a good amount of my pain, so I went with him several times until I found out it was a clinic for heroin addicts to get off the drug. I freaked out because I was not an addict, I never even used heroin. I took a small amount of pain pills for my pain, not to get high as he did. Steven was happy, he said, "It makes me high." Every time we went there, he increased his dose until he topped out at 100mg. After I found out what this place was, I reduced my dose until I was off of it. He continued to go for about a year before he went back to the pain pills.

After doing nails at The Nail Shack for about a year, my sister Pam helped me get a job as a manicurist at the salon at the Excalibur Hotel & Casino on the Las Vegas Strip. I loved my job at the Excalibur and worked there for about two years before going to work at the Luxor's salon. Steven still made me give him my money, but I was making a lot more and was able to stash more away for when I might need it. While I was working and we had the dogs, things between us were pretty good. There was not much physical abuse because he needed my money from working. If he hurt me, I would miss work and he was all about my money. There was still a lot of verbal abuse; I guess he needed to keep me under his control. I knew that it would only be a matter of time before he would lash out at me again. After work, I would usually spend some time with the dogs and then hide in my bedroom. I never told anyone at work that I was a victim of domestic violence. Feeling that they couldn't or wouldn't help me made it seem useless to tell anyone. That was a mistake because someone could've done something.

I continued to suffer from the hives with breakouts every few days when he would verbally abuse me or show his temper. My back was in constant pain because of the position I needed to be in to do pedicures, but working was my salvation. It kept me in the real world and I felt like I had some kind of a life.

I had been working at the Luxor for a few years now and we were as happy as I thought we could be. With both of us working we decided to buy a house. Steven didn't want to go look at houses and told me to go and find a nice one. He informed me what he wanted the house to have, a good size yard, two-car garage and a pool. I went with the realtor and told her what we wanted in the house. The first house looked haunted, it had dark walls and a gloomy feeling. The pool was big enough for a Barbie doll. I fell down walking up to the next house, which was a bad sign so we left. The third was nice, it had a pool and I told the realtor, "I like this house, I hope it has purple carpet."

She laughed and said, "Good Luck!"

The realtor almost fainted when we walked into the house because the carpet was purple. The house was pretty and very clean. The street had a cool name, Golden Sage. It felt right to me. The owner's, Jim And Tammy were getting a divorce. I wondered if it was another sign. We purchased the house and I thought maybe things were changing for the better. The last house was all about breeding dogs and saving to buy our own house. However, the verbal abuse never stopped nor did the lying. I did all I could to make our marriage better. I worked and took care of him. I did the laundry, cleaned the house only to have him go through and mess it up just after I finished cleaning it. It felt as though we were friends more than husband and wife. There was no romance in our marriage; I never received any hugs or kisses. Our sex life deteriorated to nothing over the years and he blamed it on his addiction to the pills for his loss of sex drive. However, we did have sex the first night in our new house.

We were excited about our new home. His mother kept telling him not to buy a house with me. She didn't like me and never gave me a chance. She felt that I was a threat from day one. His Grandmother, Helen, who has since passed away, and I really liked each other. She told me that Steven's mother felt that I was going to take him away from her. That was something I never intended to do. But, when two people get married, they need to come together as one and form a sacred bond.

A bond that is strong with love and trust. Steven's father and I had a good relationship. He told Steven that I was the best thing that ever happened to him.

Steven was still working at Whiskey Pete's Casino in Stateline, NV. He hated the 40-minute drive to work. One day he came to me and told me that he had a surprise. His old supervisor offered him a job at a new casino that was being built called The Venetian. He was so happy and proud of himself and it made me feel happy. I asked him, "Are they going to have a spa?"

He said, "Yes, but I don't know anyone in the Spa and can't help you get a job there."

I told him, "I will apply and see what happens."

"It's going to be a high end casino and you will not get the job! You're not good enough" he responded. He was trying to discourage me from trying to get a job there. It seemed that he didn't want us to work in the same casino. He probably felt that he might lose his hold on me if I began working there, as I would be around different people all day and talk to them. I found out that the spa was called Canyon Ranch Spa Club. One night I had a dream that I was doing nails there. He told me, "You're dream was wrong! You're crazy if you think you will get hired there." My co-workers at the Luxor thought I was crazy as well. I was not about to let anyone talk me out of trying.

I pursued my dream and was called for an interview. My excitement was incredible. My interview went well. However, four thousand other people applied for the position as well so my chances were slim. To my surprise, I was called back for an audition. They informed me that I needed to bring a model to work on, my mother happily agreed to be my model.

The audition was held at the Gold Coast Casino Spa. They informed us that we would only get to see the Canyon Ranch Spa if we were hired to work there. I quickly became very nervous. What made me more nervous was the fact that I was the first to audition. While doing my mother's nails, the person watching me asked, "Are you nervous?"

I replied, "Yes, Very. This means a lot to me."

She replied, "You don't look nervous at all." When I finished, she shook my hand and said, "Thank you. We'll be in touch."

Three weeks went by and I didn't hear anything. Steven was rubbing it in everyday. Laughing at me for trying and putting me down. He said, "Who are you kidding? There is no way you are good enough to work there! You are not that lucky!"

About four weeks after my audition, we were at home, the phone rang and I answered it. The man on the other end said, "I am George L, The Director of the Spa at Canyon Ranch." My heart stopped and I sat there unsure of what to say. He continued, "We would like to offer you a full-time position as a nail tech in the salon."

I almost fainted. My dream of working there had come true. Quickly, I said, "Yes, I would love to accept the position. Thank you. I am so excited."

He laughed and said, "I wish the other's were as excited as you are."

When I hung up the phone, I ran out and told Steven. His jaw dropped, he was speechless. After a moment he said, "Oh my God! Do you know what this means for your career?"

Excitedly, I responded, "I know."

He continued, "I'm proud of you. You are going to make us a lot of money!"

After I was given the job, we were taken on a tour of the Spa. I instantly fell in love with the environment it had a warm feeling of relaxation with soft lighting. Each nail station was beautifully handmade of wood and the floors were black, gold and maroon marble. Each nail station had gold silk curtains for privacy if the customer requested it. I scored the highest on my interviews, so I was given first choice of station. I took the first one on the right side, next the nail polish and the sink that looked like a waterfall. One reason I took this station was that it was closest to the front and my walk would be a little shorter.

They selected seven nail techs; I later found out that I was the only one that was not juiced in. "Juiced in" is when someone pulls some strings for you to get a job. I was proud of myself and saw this as a second chance at life. No longer was I going to be trapped in this life with him. I could make enough money to be able leave him and support myself. I knew he was never going to change. He continued to control my every move; I had little if any freedom.

The other girls that I worked with started becoming my friends. They started inviting me to their get togethers. Unfortunately, Steven would not allow me to join them. Only once did he allow me to go to one of their birthday dinners. I think he might have felt that if I was able to get close to them, I might tell them about my life at home. If so, he might have been right. He was still abusive towards me, even though I was working; it was just not as bad as it had been in the past.

The first year at Canyon Ranch, I made a lot of money. I felt like a machine, working hard everyday while enduring the pain in my back and fighting the hives just to come home and have him take the money I had just made. One thing that was good was that we purchased two brand new cars. I bought a blue 1999 Chevrolet Camero. He bought a 1999 Pontiac Grand-Am. We paid for them with the money I was making. I hated that he took my money, but at least I had my own car.

It was hard on my body working in the salon. I would do about ten manicures and ten pedicures a day. At the end of a busy day it was hard for me to stand up straight. My back was in so much pain it was unreal. I was worried about how long I could continue to keep up the pace. My co-workers knew something was wrong with me physically, but I never told them I was abused at home. I needed to keep my job so that I would be able to leave him, if I could!

The owner of The Venetian's secretary, Alma started getting her nails done at the salon. She would always request me to do her nails and we became friends. As our friendship developed, she invited me to her house for lunch. I accepted and opened up to her about my life. She told me, "You need to leave him! Have trust in your faith that God has blessed you and will continue to do so." As she told me that, I knew she was right, but I was afraid to leave him and still had nowhere to go. I remembered what she said and hoped that someday I would have the strength and the ability to leave him. My self-esteem was low and there were not enough people around me that could boost my self-esteem.

Chapter 9
Matt C.

My stress at work escalated when we were told that the owners of Canyon Ranch were going to come in and we were going to be tested. The night before, I couldn't sleep. A thousand things kept going through my head. What if I fall behind on my time? What if I make a mistake? What if I have a severe hive attack? What if I lose my job? How would I tell Steven? And how bad would he hurt me? As these thoughts continued, time slowly crept by. Sleep was sporadic at best.

At 7 a.m., my alarm went off and it was time to get ready. I took a quick shower, curled my hair and put on my make-up. I wanted to look my best for the owners so I took a little more time. As I went out of the bedroom, Steven was sleeping on the couch like normal. I was quiet while leaving as not to wake him up. My nerves were a mess and I didn't need any grief from him.

When I arrived at work, I prepared my station for the day ahead as normal. I always try to do my best and was very professional at it. Being proud of myself for getting this job, I took great pride in my work. It was very busy so I didn't really notice the owners being there much. As the day went on, the stress eased a bit. The owners came and watched everything for a while and left. They seemed pleased with the way the salon was running.

It was now 4:30 and I was exhausted and drained. With getting little sleep, my back pain and the hives, I was running on empty. It felt like there was a lot on my shoulders. I looked at the clock and took a deep breath and headed to the front desk to check my schedule, hoping that I was done for the day. As I approached the desk I noticed a man sitting in the waiting area. He seemed to be staring a hole right through me, it felt like he was waiting for me and knew who I was. He was cute and I looked away.

Arriving at the desk, I saw I had one more client on the book. The name was scribbled and I couldn't read it. I asked the receptionist, "What does that say?"

She looked at it and said, "His last name is Cohen."

Turning around, I looked at the man sitting across the room that had been staring at me and said, "Are you Mr. Cohen?"

He nodded his head "Yes" and stood up smiling as he began to walk towards me. As he approached me he said, "You can call me Matt." He was very tall, I am 5'9" and he towered over me. He had a great body; dark hair and big sparkling brown eyes. The way he gazed into my eyes took my breath away. He was the most beautiful and amazing man I had ever seen in my life. I was instantly attracted to him and there was a warm comforting feeling around us.

I said, "Come with me," as I turned and motioned for him to follow me back to the pedicure room. We walked towards my station as he followed me. When we arrived at my station, I said, "Have a seat right here," as I pointed towards the chair. He wouldn't sit; he just stood face to face with me staring deep into my eyes. Feeling a little awkward, I looked away. However, I could hear him communicating with me telepathically. He was saying, "Don't look away from me. Do you know who I am?" So my eyes slowly began to look back at him. First, I looked at his chest then up to his chin, mouth, nose and finally his eyes. When our eyes met they were locked together. I stared deep into his big sparkling brown eyes and he was staring back deep into my green eyes. Feeling him look deep into my soul, I was melting under his warm glaze. I was nervous as it felt as though I knew him. I saw flashes of light and flashes of gold. Our souls had completely merged together and we were one. It was the most unconditional love I had ever felt in my life. I began to see flashes of past lives that we shared together. It was like we had come full circle and met in this lifetime.

We stared at each other for what seemed to be an eternity, but in reality was about 10 minutes before I came out of the trance we were in. I had fallen head over heals in love with him. For the first time in my life I felt true unconditional love.

He finally sat down and I began his pedicure. I had no idea how I was going to be able to concentrate. I told him, "Put your feet in the water."

As he began to put his feet in, he quickly pulled them out and said, "Baby, the water's too hot." I quickly apologized and fixed the problem, however there was only a feeling of love around us. He just looked into my eyes and smiled. He began asking me a lot of questions. I also asked him some, but unfortunately not enough. He told me many things about himself; he loved basketball and was moving from New York to Los Angeles to pursue a career in Television.

Every time he smiled at me, a happy, warm feeling came over me. He had the most wonderful smile I had ever seen with perfect white teeth. I was so nervous, but calm at the same time. He was like a sculpture. I paid attention to every fiber of his being. It felt as though I was washing the feet of Jesus. It was divine intervention.

As I massaged his feet and calves, I wanted him to feel my love for him. He looked at me with a smile that could light up the darkest of rooms. Then he closed his eyes and accepted my embrace of love through my touch.

The hour I spent giving him his pedicure seemed to fly by. As I finished up, I didn't want it to end. I reluctantly walked him to the front and said, " I hope you'll come back and see me," as I gave him my card and again we looked deep into each other's eyes. He took his hand and touched my wrist, gently sliding his hand over my hand until he reached my card. His fingers gently took a hold of my card as he said, "I will be back!" as I turned and began to walk away.

He said, "Don't go!" Instantly, I gasp and my heart stopped. I turned around as he was walking towards me. He reached out his hand and handed me a tip. For a split second, I thought and hoped that he was going to ask me to go away with him.

After he left, I was exhilarated. He lit a fire in my spirit and new life into me. For the first time in a long time, I was happy. I can't explain it, but he gave me strength and courage. That one-hour with Matt seemed to change my life. I began to feel better about myself and started to believe that there was hope after all. What I experienced with him was love at first sight. I could feel myself glowing and knew that he would come back someday.

Before Matt, I was dead inside and felt that my life meant little and I would be with Steven forever. He changed that feeling and gave me hope for the future. He was all I could think about and I thought God must have sent him to save me. God did send him there to breath life and love back into me. Matt gave me back the self-confidence that I had completely lost. Steven had me convinced that he was the only man that would ever want to be with me. Now here was this wonderful and beautiful man that showed me love. He showed me that I was still beautiful and other men would find me attractive. I loved him and knew that without a doubt he loved me just as much. My self-esteem was going through the roof.

Never would I think about cheating on my husband, my wedding vows are very sacred to me. For better or worse, till death do us part, that's part of the reason I stayed with Steven even with the physical, mental and verbal abuse. But, if Matt would've asked me to go away with him, I would've dropped everything in the blink of an eye and gone.

I was excited about seeing him again and believed he would come back for me. He never did return in the physical, but it was all right. He had carried me through the years that followed and I cried many tears with his name on them. In my times of darkness and despair I would think of him and he would give me strength. There were countless times when I felt despair and would think of him and rejoice in the love we shared. I would go to my car and listen to music and I could feel him there with me and it was an incredible feeling. He lifted my spirit and I now know that he was an Angel sent from God to save me and breathe life and hope back into me. I know that I will see him again one day and thank him for saving me. I believe he is now in Heaven because he comes to me in my dreams and they are very clear. He continues to guide me today and I know that he loves me universes full. In my mind, body and spirit, I know who he is and I am honored to be loved so much by him. Thank you Matt C. my heart will forever have a place for you.

Chapter 10
Trying To Find My Way Back To Myself

Continuing to work was becoming more and more difficult. Between the stress at home and at work my hives were unbearable. My body was beginning to break down. At home, Steven continued to lie to me about everything. It seemed that everything he said was a lie. All I asked was for him to be honest and tell me the truth. How could we possibly have a lasting relationship without being honest with each other? There were cigarette butts everywhere outside of the house, in the front yard and the backyard. He would swear on my life, his life, and other people's lives that he was telling the truth and they were not his.

One day, I went to the grocery store, which was the only place he ever allowed me to go without him. Just after leaving the house, I realized that I had forgotten the grocery list and needed to go back and get it. Upon returning home, I noticed he was standing out back. I went to see what he was doing and saw him smoking. Before I could even say a word, he looked at me and instantly became irate. His face lost all expression and quickly turned red. It appeared he was angry that I returned so early and caught him outside smoking. He burst into the house like a mad man, screaming and yelling at me. I began to retreat towards my bedroom, which I called "The Dungeon", for safety. He caught me in the dining room and grabbed my arm and spun me around. Before I had a chance to get my balance, he hit me with his fist and broke my nose and gave me a black eye. I fell to the ground and as quickly as I could stood up and continued towards the dungeon for safety. He was in a tirade, throwing anything and everything in his path that he could get his hands on every which way. He grabbed our computer that was set up on the dining room table, picked it up and threw it to the ground breaking it into several pieces and then he kicked over two of the chairs.

When I reached the bedroom, I was confused and relieved at the fact that he was not right behind me as he usually was and it was relatively quiet. I waited several minutes before slowly emerging from the bedroom to see what had happened. I thought that he might have left. I was stunned and taken back when I found him. He had crawled under the table and curled up into the fetal position. He was crying. When he saw me standing there, he said, "I'm scared!" Being confused and not knowing what to say, I didn't say anything back to him. I think it was his way of getting me to feel sorry for him, at the time it worked. I just turned and walked back to the bedroom, as I wanted him to leave me alone.

At the time, I thought that he might have a mental illness, but now I think it was just another way of him keeping me under his control. He probably figured that if I thought he was mentally ill that I wouldn't call the police on him and have him arrested. It worked, as I felt sorry for him as I closed the door to my bedroom, climbed into bed and pulled the sheets over me.

After he would physically or mentally abuse me, he would never say he was sorry or anything. Most of the time he would act as though it never even happened. In my opinion, verbal abuse is worse than physical abuse. The bruises go away, but the verbal and mental abuse stays and damages your self-esteem and mental state of mind.

In this time frame, there was about a month where I was happy. It is sad that in my entire marriage that there is only one time that I can remember being happy. During this month, I had no torment from Steven. At night, he left me alone and I was getting a full night sleep without being woken up several times. I had a job and felt productive. I would sit on the couch in my pajamas and made objects out of clay. It was a hobby of mine since I was a little girl. I made little people, houses, fairies, angels, and even happy little neighborhoods. Steven was proud of my clay objects and told me that I should sell them. He wanted me to open a little stand and sell them. This made me feel good that he was proud of me for once in our marriage. Unfortunately, this didn't last long.

There were several times he had sent me flowers at work. This is about as romantic as he ever had been, except the only thing is that the card on the flowers would read, "Job well done" and not something romantic like, "I Love You!" It was as though I was working for him, all he seemed to care about was the money I made. We both worked at the Venetian together for four years and he never came and had lunch with me or even come up to say, "Hi!"

The next morning I woke up covered in hives, there were red itchy blotches all over my body. I had to work, so I covered the black eye with make-up and put on a black turtleneck to cover the hives. It was miserable as the hives were itching and to make matters worse, it was the middle of the summer. He was sleeping on the couch as I left for work. I didn't say anything to him, because I feared what his mood or temper would be and I didn't want to be late or lose my job.

At work it was hot. The hives continued to get worse and my face began to swell. The doctors told me that if the hives are on my lips my throat can swell and cut off my airway and I could suffocate. If my throat began to swell, I would need to use the Epi-Pen and call an ambulance. In fear of that, I asked my supervisor if I could leave work early. She said, "There's nothing wrong with you. You're faking it, you just want to get out of work!"

Suffering the way I was, I reached up and pulled the neck of my turtleneck down and showed her the hives on my neck and said, "Do you think this is faking it?"

She turned white as a ghost and said, "Oh my God! Skin things freak me out."

I replied, "Well, you shouldn't have accused me of lying."

She then asked me, "Why don't you go to lunch and come back?""

I said, "I'm sorry, but they will not go away for a while." My hives would last anywhere from several hours to several days depending on how bad my stress was.

Finally, she told to me, "Go home and rest." Even though I know she still didn't want me to leave.

After this incident, I reduced my work schedule, as I knew I could no longer keep up the pace of a ten-hour day. My health was getting worse and worse. The pain in my back was hard to handle, especially when I had to be crunched over most of the day doing pedicures. It was hard and I knew that my days of being able to do my job were numbered. I found out about a medical leave that allowed me to be able to stay home from work for a day or several days at a time if needed for medical reasons, it was called Family Medical Leave (FMLA). My doctor set it up and this made it easier to get through my reduced workweek.

Nobody that worked with me had the hives and they didn't understand them. They controlled everything about my life and interfered with my job. I kept my hives hidden as much as possible and didn't let anyone know how much I was suffering. At times, I wanted to give up, but I knew that God had a plan for me. I just had to keep my faith, which was very hard at times.

I loved my job, even though the pain it caused me was incredible at times. It made me feel very good and proud to be able to make other people feel and look good. I would get compliment cards and letters of thanks from my guests. However, Canyon Ranch was not so nice to me. I was practically forced to work with the hives as they scheduled guests throughout my workday. When my back was in pain and I could hardly walk, it was overlooked by the management.

New management took over and I thought it might get better for me, I was wrong. It seemed like I could do nothing right. My work was important to me, I needed to give the guest the best manicure or pedicure that I could. If I went a few minutes over, I would be reprimanded. The stress there was increasing; it felt as if the military had taken over the salon! The entire time I worked at Canyon Ranch, never did I receive a guest complaint. My guest's were my number one priority; they deserved the best treatment I could give them. There were several times when I had to work with the hives and was not allowed to go home that the guest's complained to the management that it was not right for them to force me to work in my condition.

A fellow manicurist had just been promoted to Lead Nail Tech. One of her first duties was to give yearly reviews. When it was my turn, she came up to me and said, "It's time for your review. Come with me." I was confused as she took me off the Canyon Ranch property and we headed into the mall at the Venetian. She had me sit down on a bench in front of the canal. It was pretty crowded and she stood over me and paced back and forth while giving me my evaluation. It was quite stressful and embarrassing as people were stopping to watch, and of course I began to break out in hives. When she was finished, she sternly said, "Now go back to work!" I was in shock; it was the worst review I had ever had. The review was not bad it was the way it was conducted. I stood up and quickly walked to the nearest restroom. I put my hands on the sink and burst into tears.

When I went home, I checked my employee handbook to see how to handle this. The handbook informed me to report the situation to the salon supervisor. First thing the next morning I reported it and she was demoted that same day. I never intended for her to be demoted, but it needed to be reported. The management never said anything to me about it, no apology was given to me, nothing! I loved my job and took great pride in my work unfortunately the management at Canyon Ranch only seemed to care about some of their employee's. I was not one of them.

Chapter 11
Held Against My Will

My health had deteriorated so badly that I had to stop working all together. This decision killed me because I loved my job, but I could no longer keep up the pace. It became impossible for me to do the simplest of tasks like the laundry and simple house cleaning. Steven was not very happy with me when I told him I was quitting my job. He didn't care about my health, only the loss of my income. It was my decision to say "Good-bye" to my job. I needed time off and it was not available so I no-called, no showed and knew that the result would be termination. I had become a burden for them even though I never received a customer complaint. My clients were always number one priority no matter how bad I was hurting. I took great pride in the job I did and was proud of my work and the satisfaction of the guest.

After I stopped working, he would often tell me how lucky I was that "He" took me out of the workplace. It was him playing a mind game on me, trying to get me to believe that I was at home because he wanted me out of the workplace. He didn't take me out of anything, my body was so broken down and abused that I had no choice but to stop working. With everything that had happened at work, I really enjoyed my job and would have liked to keep it. I was proud and happy to make my guests feel relaxed and look good.

Knowing that letting go of my security was a mistake, I had no other choice. My body needed to rest and recover. I felt like a failure because I could not keep up the pace. I am only human and didn't have a battery pack to keep me going. I was only one person trying to keep it together. Now I needed to rely completely on him, there was no more independence for me. I was totally dependent on him!

Every time my spirit faded, I would pray to God that someday soon he would bring Matt back into my life. That one-hour with him never left my heart or thoughts. In my worst despair I always found myself thinking of him. The hope that one-day he would come back and save me from the hell I was trapped in is what kept me going.

I couldn't stand the torture Steven was putting me through, both verbally and physically. I decided to go back to work, even though my body was in no shape to be there. I managed to get my old job back doing nails at the salon at the Luxor. However, this was short lived as the hive attacks and my back pain made it too hard to do. My nail career was over.

Most of my time was now spent in the dungeon. Steven kept me pinned in there, he would sometimes put a big heavy box in front of the door that I was unable to move and therefore was trapped. The only times that I would be allowed out was when he would take me to the doctor for more pills. He continually ordered me not to tell anyone what was happening at home or he would kill me. I had little hope, but still didn't want to die so I kept his secret. No longer was I his wife, now I was his prisoner.

He owned fifteen guns now, assault rifles, shotguns and handguns. They were loaded and scattered around the house. I often thought that they would be my fate. Ever since the mistaken identity, he felt that he needed to be able to protect himself and home from invasion by intruders and police.

In the pictures you can see his SKS rifle leaning against the couch where he slept, one of his semi-auto pistols on the white table by the remote controls. These were not there to be cleaned as you can see there are no cleaning materials around.

In the first picture, the gun is on the white table in the foreground.

My physician, Dr. DeShazo never knew what was happening at home. He knew about my ailments, but didn't know they were caused by domestic violence. He always asked us a lot of questions about our health and how we were feeling, but Steven was always in the room with me and I had to answer the questions the way I was told to. Dr. DeShazo also confirmed that I had Post-Traumatic Stress Syndrome when I told him, "I feel like a P.O.W. returning from war on a helicopter."

At home, my life was getting worse. Steven was controlling everything. He would not let me go into the kitchen. He put a black cord across the floor in the living room just about knee height to alert him if I tried to get something to eat. I had gained weight because I was taking steroids for the hives.

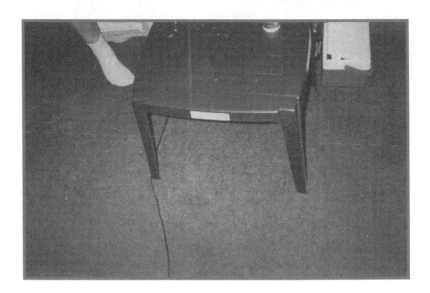

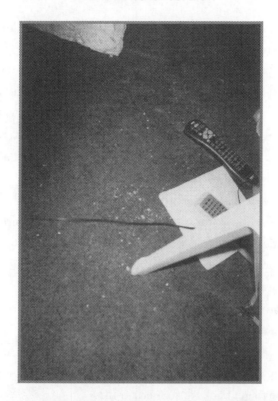

In the first two pictures the cord is laying on the ground. In the third picture the cord is on the ground behind me. It was taken on one of the few occasions when I was allowed out of the dungeon. I'm petting Bon Bon in this picture.

He said, "You're fat and need to lose weight." I was not eating much, but the steroids caused me to put on about eighty pounds. My weight was about 220 pounds. I was also prescribed diet pills to help me lose weight. The only thing he would allow me to eat was frozen macaroni and cheese. He would always make me eat it in front of him. It always looked funny and I would question him about it. He said, "I have a special way of cooking it." But he cooked it in the microwave! It had a brown glaze crust like it would have if it were cooked in the oven. There was a funny taste and it had little black specks on it, which he said was pepper. I knew what pepper looked like and this was not pepper, but what could I do? If I refused to eat it, I might not have been given anything else or he might have become angry and hurt me. When I asked him to taste it he would say, "It's not for me, it's for you!" and he never tasted it! There were several times when I tried to get something to eat from the kitchen and was tripped by that cord. Instead of being nice to me, he would laugh at me and tell me to get back in the bedroom.

Now that my mind is free and clear, I believe he was drugging it or something. All my life I had a pretty good memory and at this time, my memory was fading fast. I was having a hard time remembering simple things. He had me believing that I was dying. He would constantly tell me that the dead brain matter and scar tissue on the right side of my brain was leaking into my bloodstream. My memory was fading so I believed him, even though no doctor ever stated that. With my memory loss, Dr. DeShazo thought I might be getting Alzheimer's disease or something.

He continued his hold on me any way he could. He controlled what I ate, what I watched on TV and whom I could talk to. I later found out that on several occasions my mother and sister Donna would come to visit. He would not let them in and told them that I was sleeping. Several of our neighbors also tried to see me with the same result, no entry! He wanted total control of everything and did his best to achieve it and for the most part, he did!

He found an old Chevrolet Nova and without asking me, he bought it. It was a piece of junk. He began restoring it and would spend hours in the garage working on it. He was taking several pain pills and also several of my diet pills now and would stay up all night. The neighbors were complaining that he was making too much noise in the middle of the night. It didn't bother him that they were angry with him. He would just say things like, "Their assholes!" or "This is my house, I can do whatever I want! I don't care what they think!"

He spent thousands of dollars on that car. If he needed a part or a tool, he just bought it. Money seemed to be no object to him. However, if I asked for something, he would say, "You don't need that!" With him spending our money on him, this made me feel like I didn't matter; only his car mattered to him. The only time he even bought me a Birthday gift was my Birthday right after we met. I had to buy my own cake every year. For Christmas, he would give me a couple of hundred dollars and say, "Go buy something." This made Christmas a sad time for me, as there were no presents to open on Christmas morning. Even though Christmas isn't about gifts, it's about the birth of Christ; it is still nice to have something to open Christmas morning.

As for how much he slept, I am not sure as he slept on the couch now. We had no sex life since we bought the house in 1999. I would never get any love or affection. He never kissed or hugged me anymore, not even a soft touch. I was very neglected. He would always say, "I love you!" but they were just words. I don't think he loved me. Love is more than words. Love is strong, not empty words!

He knew that I had saved some money while I was working, but he didn't know how much. I had no intention of sharing it with him, as it was my safety net if he left me again. It was all I had, my only hope if I needed to leave him or if he left me.

One afternoon he approached me in the dungeon and asked, "How much money do you have stashed?"

I asked, "Why do you ask?"

He said, "I need more parts and don't have the money."

"I don't have much and it's for an emergency." I exclaimed to him.

"Bitch, How much fucking money do you have?" he yelled and continued to verbally abuse me by calling me every horrible name in the book. I stood up and headed towards the bathroom to get away from the abuse. He lunged at me and threw me to the ground. Landing on the tile floor of the bathroom with him on top of me, he grabbed my hair and pulled my head up and then slammed it onto the tile. My head was throbbing and all I could see were stars. I thought for sure that he had just re-fractured my skull, my head was not supposed to take any blows. Then he wrapped his hands around my neck and began to strangle me. He said, "You're going to die, Bitch!" as he squeezed tighter and tighter. I could not breath, I thought this time he was not going to stop. I'm going to die, it felt like I was going to pass out and then he let go. As he was getting up, he spit in my face and said, "This time you got lucky!" Something would come over him and I had to deal with the Devil.

The lies continued it was one lie after another. He would lie to me so much that he began to get his lies confused. He was lost in his life of lies. I know that he was a pathological liar.

Fearing one day soon that he would kill me, I began to take pictures of the hell I was living in. I wanted and needed the truth to be able to come out someway, somehow even if through my death. It felt as though there was not much left of me and the pictures would show the scattered pieces of the destruction of me. At this point, all I had left was my faith that God would help me free myself of this horrible nightmare.

Steven walked into the dungeon and had a glare in his eyes that screamed "Evil". I was terrified at what was about to come. He began yelling at me, saying many horrible things and calling me names. He began to grab my small items off the dresser and throwing them at me as hard as he could. As he was throwing my things at me he began to smile as though he was enjoying it. He then said, "Looks like I win!" To this day, I do not know what he meant by that.

Not being able to take it any longer, I looked him straight in the eyes as I sat up. He stopped throwing my things at me as I reached over to the nightstand and picked up his loaded .357 that was always there. I pointed the gun at my head. I was now at the lowest point of my life. There was no way I could get any closer to the ground. It didn't matter to me if I lived or died. No matter what I tried to do to make things better, nothing worked. There was no getting through to him and the madness and abuse wouldn't stop. I felt I had nothing to lose as I had pretty much lost it all already.

As I held the gun to my head with my finger on the trigger I said to him, "What is it going to take to get you to stop torturing me? Maybe I should just blow my head off before you do, is that what you want?" He just stood there and stared into my eyes. I could feel the vibe; it was almost like he was saying, "Yes, do it!" He had no reaction of fear. He just stood there with a stone cold face.

As I continued to hold the gun to my head, I saw a flash in my head of Jesus on the cross. It felt as though Jesus was telling me not to let him win. As this flashed in my head, I stated to Steven, "Nope, I win. You're not worth me taking my life. Here, you can have your gun back!" as I laid the gun down on the bed beside me. He slowly walked over towards the bed with a frightened look on his face, maybe he saw the God in me. He picked up the gun and walked out of the room. I was disappointed in myself for allowing him to get me to that point. He striped me of everything but my faith and now I was his prisoner. I knew suicide was not the answer but I was at a point where it didn't matter to me either way.

What is nothing?

Nothing is when you look inside
So deep you're almost afraid to go there
When I'm there, what do I see?
I see nothing!
On the outside looking in

You see so much
The envy of everyone
"Why can't I be that lucky," they say
"Wish I had a man like that!"
When I come inside
What do I see?
It's cold, it's hollow, and it's empty
With so many years together
There should be so much inside
Why is there nothing?
It's hollow there is no substance
It's just the idea that it's so great
That holds it together
Love, What is love to you?
Love is when you look in my eyes
So deep and lie to my soul
Is love a security blanket for you?
That allows you to trample on my heart
Love to me is much more than that
It's exposing one's weakness and strengths
Sharing and surviving the storms
Love is honesty
You and I know no honesty
We've been around the circles
Time and time again
Wasting years, wasting life
Love is warmth and intimacy
If you have a marriage
That has no embrace of a touch
Or the warmth from a hug
The only other way for me of intimacy
Would be honesty
We have neither

That's what I mean when I say
"There's Nothing!"

There were many other reasons for me to get away from him. Before he stabbed me, he told me that he once had a dream that he stabbed his grandmother to death. It scared me, but I let it pass. His grandmother has already passed by the time he told me about it, but it still scared me. Also, when he was nine years old, he planted a bomb that he made in a library full of children and set it off. I didn't believe him and he told me to ask his father. The next time we went to see his father, I did ask and his father showed me the folder with the police report and the newspaper article. Luckily, no body was hurt and he didn't get in much trouble because his father was a high-ranking military official. This confirmed to me that I was with someone that had to have serious mental problems.

Steven invited his mother to come visit us. It would be the first time she had come to our house in the four years we had been there. She had just married a much older man named Milton. He was a very nice man that was suffering from Alzheimer's.

When his mother and her husband, Milton arrived at our house, I was in the bedroom getting weaker by the day. Steven and Milton were in the living room and his mother came into the bedroom. She entered the room and didn't say a word as she shut the door behind her, which confused me. She quickly came over to the bed and jumped onto it next to me and started grilling me about my life. This was a weird and uncomfortable act as she didn't say "Hello" or have any small talk. At first I was answering her questions and then I asked her, "Why are you doing this?"

She sternly replied, "Just answer the questions." I was startled and tried to get up and she would not let me. Grabbing my arm and pulled me back down while saying, "Stay right where you are and tell me everything." She asked me specific questions about my car accident I had at eighteen, wanting to know the street names and other driver's involved, what hospital I went to, ect. Over and over I was questioned about everything in my life. This continued for about five hours, I was not allowed to get up, have a drink, or even go to the bathroom. I kept praying that my husband would come in and put a stop to this, but he never came. She would not stop and to this day, I still don't know the point of it all. She entered the room just after noon and left around five p.m.

When she finally left the room, Milton came in to see me. I was scared and traumatized by what had just happened. Lying there in bed, it felt like I was dying. He asked me, "Is there anything I can do for you?"

In a soft voice, I replied, "Please, get me out of here!" Unfortunately, he never did anything for me, probably because of the Alzheimer's or that Steven's mother had complete control of him both mentally and financially. That was the extent of their visit as they left shortly after that and went to dinner. Steven and I were not invited to accompany them.

For several weeks he continued to only let me eat the frozen macaroni and cheese that he made for me. Every time he brought it to me, he sat next to me and made me eat every bit of it. At this point, he was taking about twenty of the pain and diet pills a day, as he had several doctors giving him the prescriptions. He would try to get me to take some with him, but I refused. Once, he threatened me and ordered me to take a pill with him. Not wanting to be hurt again, I took a pill he gave me. It was one of the diet pills and it made me feel weird. I am not positive, but I think that is what he was putting in my food.

The next time he talked to his mother, he told me that she wanted to put me in a home so that he didn't need to take care of me. He said that his mother would pay for it and that they both thought it would be the best thing for me. This scared me and made me angry. Scared because I didn't want to be hidden away from my mother and the few people I was allowed to talk to. I was also angry because he was my husband and supposed to take care of me, even though he was more of a captor and I his prisoner. I was treated more like an animal than his wife.

He had me convinced that the brain matter was leaking into my body and that was why my memory was fading and why I was so weak. A doctor DID NOT diagnose this. I begged him, "Please don't put me in a home." I don't know why, but luckily I was not put away.

Somewhere in this time, I began to pick at my skin. I felt trapped and depressed that this was my life. I would pick my skin mostly in the chest area until it bled. When he would see what I was doing, he would tell me, "Stop picking your skin." I have no idea why I did that to myself. It was bad, once the sore would start to heal I would pick at it again. I became someone that I didn't know!

My depression worsened and I began to give up on life. I was ready to die. I still had my faith that God would deliver me, but I had lost all hope. I had blonde hair that went all the way down to my lower back. It was beautiful and I normally took good care of it. I stopped brushing it and it became badly tangled. Steven took me to the hairdresser to try to fix it. After about an hour, they said, "It's a lost cause." Then they asked, "Do you want us to cut it off for you?"

I was very saddened when I heard her say that. Looking at the ground, I said, "No, I'll do it myself" as I tried to hold back my tears. We went home and I went into the shower to cut it off myself. As I was cutting my hair off, I was picturing all the years of hell I had been through being cut away. My hair was now short, like a man's hairstyle. I loved my long hair and now it was gone. It took me years to grow it as long as it was.

His verbal abuse continued and everyday he would say demeaning things to me like, "You're not attractive", "You're fat and ugly", "I'm the only man that would ever want to be with you" or "No man will think you are pretty." I believed him and thought I would die in that bed. I felt no love from him; it had been years since we last had sex. He never embraced, held, kissed or touched me in a loving way anymore.

Chapter 12
The Final Year With Steven

Things in my life were continuing to get worse. I was gradually slipping away from reality. My doctors couldn't figure out what was wrong with me and kept giving me pain prescriptions along with other medications to try and help me. I was beginning to surrender to the fact that my health was failing me and my life was ending. Steven had me convinced it was the end of my life and the doctors seemed unable to help me.

With my back hurting severely, I had to walk with a cane. I made an appointment with my dermatologist and Steven took me, of course. When he parked the car, he climbed out and walked to the front of the car and stood there. Looking at me as I tried to get out, he said, "Hurry up!"

I asked him, "Can you help me?"

He just laughed at me and said, "No, Do it yourself."

As we walked up to the door, he opened it and walked thru letting the door close behind him. He didn't open it for me or hold it open so I could get in. The Gentleman behind me was nice enough to open it for me. I was so emotionally hurt and embarrassed by the way he had just treated me. Everyone in the waiting room just stared at him with the look of disgust, but it didn't bother him. The feeling I had was so eerie yet comforting as people were seeing the monster he was. I realized that I didn't know him anymore, not even a small part of him that I thought I would always know. It felt like I was looking at a complete stranger! He had not been my husband in some time and now he was no longer even my friend. All I saw was a blank stare with no soul inside. He was probably high on pills as his eyes were glazed over.

Sometimes in the past after he would abuse me physically, he would feel a twinge of guilt and would ask me what I wanted. I would try to get him to be nice to me, but it would only last a day or so. Now, I would just ask him for money to buy a new wedding ring to replace the one I had to sell when he left me with nothing. It was hurtful that he wouldn't buy me a ring to show his love for me and that I needed to buy my own. He told me to buy a fake one until I could afford a real ring. It should have been a sign that his love was not real. So, I told him it was my plan to save money for a ring, but in reality it was for my stash, which was several thousand dollars at that point.

My depression was worsening and Dr. De Shazo put me on Prozac for my Post-Traumatic Distress Syndrome, which made my depression worse. We then tried several different prescriptions to find one that worked. However, we couldn't find anything that did anything for my depression or my PTDS so I stopped taking anything for it.

For the most part life was becoming extremely hard, not just physically but also mentally. There wasn't much fight left in me, it was a hopeless situation getting worse. I always put my life in God's hands and believe I had defied the odds more than a few times already in my life. After all I had been thru in my life by this point, people would often tell me that it's a miracle that I'm alive and that I didn't rely on things or substances to numb me from all the pain. There were times I hated my life so much I would have welcomed an escape from reality. However, I restrained myself.

When I would come out of the dungeon and peek around the corner to see what he was doing, he would be sitting on the couch stoned and so numb to life that he was feeling no pain. I would feel both sorry for him and ashamed of him at the same time. I needed to be quiet because I never knew what mood he would be in if he would've woken up. He would usually be passed out on the couch with his food all over him.

One time, he had a bowl of Frosted Mini Wheat that had tipped over and spilled on his chest. The milk had dripped down his torso and legs, his eyes were closed and he was oblivious to what had happened. Two hours later, I came back out of the room and he was still out of it. The cereal was dried up and sticking to his body, it was a big mess! I would often take a picture of him thinking I would show him and let him see what he had become.

There were times when I would be in gridlock with my physical pain and hardly able to walk with my back that I just wanted to escape my pain for a while. On two different occasions I tried to feel what it was that those pills did for him. I took four of them at one time wishing my back would stop hurting for a while. To my surprise, those four pills didn't faze me a bit, no relief from the pain, no feeling of being high, not even a yawn.

There was no escaping my pain. In my heart I believe that God has a plan for all of us and I knew that there must be a bigger plan for me than this. I just didn't know what it was, but I felt that I was going to help people in this world somehow! I thought that if people knew what I had been through their problems might not seem too bad and they could overcome them. I thought that if I survived, my story might teach people a lesson and keep them out of my situation. When you feel as though you have nothing and your in total aloneness, if you have that special someone to love you, a place to rest your head, food to eat, and family that cares about you, then you really have a lot!

I was so isolated from life, people, friends and family that when it came down to it, I had no one. There was no one there for me except Jesus. Everyday, I wished someone would come and rescue me from it all. Just to have someone to wrap their arms around me and let me cry on their shoulder would have meant the world to me. Steven would often tell me, "Crying is a sign of weakness." Therefore I was not allowed to cry. When I was locked in the room I could not cry, fearing that he might walk in and catch me crying and get angry. I had forgotten the relief you feel from that cry.

It was now about two years after I stopped working and he was still going on and on about how grateful I should be to him that "He" took me out of the workplace. He constantly wanted my praise and for me to bow to him as my savior. He was anything but my savior. It wasn't him that stopped me from working; it was what he did to my body and the hives that forced me out. I was so physically broken the pace had become too much for my body to keep up with. And after four years working at Canyon Ranch, I could do no more. I had nothing left. I really should have stopped working when he first herniated the disk in my back. When the hives covered my face and body, it was my spirit saying enough is enough. The stress of my home life and working was too much for my body to process and it was affecting me physically.

In the Dungeon I would listen to Christian music over and over again and watch church on television. That would take me away from my life of hell for a while, but something wasn't right. I felt like I was doing Jesus, the only Father I have ever known, a complete injustice. I was wasting away into a vegetable and was feeling spiritually dead inside. I would pray to God that if he would give me just one more chance at life, one chance to get it right and make a difference in this world, I would. I prayed if I could survive this misery, he could use me as a tool, an example to help people learn about abuse.

In my heart I believe that God chose me for this mission of domestic violence awareness because he knew I was strong enough and take from a bad experience something to make life better for someone else. Many people tell me that it is amazing that I am not an alcoholic or hooked on heroin or cocaine. I can't numb myself, I need to be strong and keep my faith. I'm fully aware of my pain, the breakdown and dysfunction of my life and the vicious cycle of abuse I had suffered. During this time talking to God and rebuilding my faith, I began to see through the fog Steven had put me in.

One afternoon I was in the Dungeon waiting on him to bring me my frozen macaroni and cheese. He was in another numb state of mind, he had ordered Chinese food and sat down on the couch to eat it. Of course

I didn't get any, I received my usual, frozen macaroni and cheese. When I went out to see what was going on, I saw him passed out with a plate full of food spilled all over him, the couch and the floor. It was a disgusting mess, so I took another picture of him along with all of the guns he had lying around. I guess a part of me figured that if he killed me the pictures would tell the story of what had happened because at this point I had no voice to the outside world.

While he was at work one day, I ventured out to the living room to get a change of scenery for a while. I stumbled upon a stack of pornography, DVD's and videotapes. He had stacks and stacks of them everywhere, I was amazed at how many there were. There were so many that I couldn't count them all. I felt betrayed; it made me feel like he cheated on me. We were married for seventeen years at this time and it had been ten years since we were last intimate together and now I knew why! I had forgotten what it felt like to be touched or kissed. He would tell me that he had no sex drive because of the pain pills he took. He would tell me, "It's not you, it's the pills." Well, he could have fooled me, because he had me believing that I was fat, unattractive and unappealing to everyone but him. Time and time again, he would make me stand on the scale to see how much I weighed. It made me believe that I was fat and nobody would ever want to be with me. Maybe it would have been better for me to be alone; at least I would have been safe.

After finding the pornography, my depression worsened. I began to pick my skin on my chest until it would bleed again. I never had a desire to cut myself or cause myself serious pain. It was kind of a release for me and it showed me that I was still alive. I didn't think anyone would ever see my chest again so I picked this area for that reason. One time he came in and caught me picking my skin and began to freak out. He started yelling at me and said, "Stop doing that and never do it again."

It was like an obsession, I could not stop once I started. I just looked at him and said, "Why? You don't care about me anyway!" Then I would tell him, "Just leave me alone."

This entire year, he would talk about quitting his job. He said that he hated working and felt as though he was to good to do hard work. He told me that he had been written up at work for being late. He would never let me see the write up form, so I knew there was more to the story than he was telling me.

His hygiene had become pathetic. He stopped taking showers before work. He just ran his hands under the water and then through his hair. It was awful; he would go to work like that and without even brushing his teeth. Trying to help him, I would do the laundry and clean the bathroom for him. I started taking a picture of the bathroom after I finished. Within minutes of me finishing, he would go into the bathroom and shave and leave it a total mess. He would leave it laughing and say to me, "Here, I gave you something to do! Clean up my mess."

It was now the summer of 2005 and I could no longer drive myself. It was becoming difficult for me to even climb out of bed. I was convinced that it was only a matter of time before I died from my brain matter leaking through my skull crack. He had stopped taking me to my doctor's appointments unless it was for pain pills. So I had to take a cab to most of my appointments.

Steven and his mother wanted to put me into a home again. This time they were serious. She told me, "I don't want my son to have to take care of you anymore. It would be best for you to be in a home."

I told her, "No, I will not go to a home. We vowed to take care of each other in our wedding vows. For better or worse!" So, I made an appointment with a neurologist to find out the extent of my illness.

Steven's mother made arrangements to have maids come and clean the house and get it in order for us. I had no say in this matter; they came in and didn't listen to anything I said. Now there were strangers going through my personnel things and putting them in boxes. Even though I told them not to pack my things they did it anyway. They were getting ready to move me into a home.

This is when I fell to my knees and began to cry and cry. I prayed to God, "I call onto you, Father God, I'm scared and I'm desperate. Please help me!

God, Please come into my life and embrace me with your love and give me the strength and wisdom so that I can regain control of my life." Not knowing what I was going to do, I knew one thing for sure. God would not leave me now. I prayed for forgiveness for all of my sins and asked for a clean start.

After a few hours passed, the doorbell rang. Steven was at work, so I answered the door. It was our neighbor, Wendy. She said, "We have not seen you in forever. How are you?" Before I could answer, she told me that her and her husband were going away to celebrate their 18th wedding anniversary. I still said nothing as she went on and on about their plans. When she finished bragging, she looked at my face and saw hives that were covering it. She than said, "What's wrong?"

I replied, "I've just been here for the last two years and have been battered and abused by my husband."

She just said, "Oh, Sorry to hear that." and she quickly left. She didn't offer to help or to call the police. At that point I knew that the only way out was for me to do it myself and not rely on help from others.

On August 5th, I was sitting at the kitchen table eating my macaroni and cheese that he made for me. It was a rare occasion that I was allowed out of the bedroom. Before I could finish eating, he walked back in and for no reason, he kicked me in the right side of my abdomen and I fell to the ground. He started yelling at me as I slowly climbed off the floor. I begged him, "Please let me go back to my room!" Because I didn't want to be hurt anymore and he was standing in the way.

He pointed me in the direction of the room and stepped out of my way and said, "Get back where you belong, Bitch!" As I walked past him, he stood there glaring at me and I expected to be hit. Thankfully, it didn't happen this time.

On August 13th, my sister Donna called me from her home in Montana. I don't know how, but I finally had the courage to tell her what had been happening to me for the last 18 years. She was stunned. In the background, she could hear him yelling and wanted me to call the police. I told her that I was too afraid of him to do it. She told me that if I wouldn't call the police she would! I thought to my self, Thank God!

We hung up the phone and I finally felt some relief. He came in the room and I told him that the police were coming. He became very angry and told me, " When they come, you keep your mouth shut! If you say anything, you will be sorry!" The tone of his voice terrified me and I fell back under his grip. I had to keep my mouth shut, just like all the other times.

Several minutes later, the doorbell rang and the police came in and demanded to talk to both of us separately. He was taken outside and they talked to me inside. After he was outside, the police looked around and saw most of his guns lying around. They asked me, "What's going on here?"

Scared of him and thinking that no one could help me, I responded, "Everything is fine."

They said, "You say that, but your eye's tell a different story. If you don't tell us, there is nothing we can do to help you."

Again, I just said, "It's fine."

As they were leaving, they told him, "You better leave her alone or next time we will take you to jail." They gave me one last look in hope of getting me to talk, but I just stood there. Watching them drive away, I knew that I had made a mistake and hoped for the best.

As he closed the door, he turned towards me and gave me an evil look that I never saw before. I slowly turned and walked back to the dungeon hoping that I would be left alone. Luckily, I was not followed and nothing was said to me. Several hours later, I opened the door and saw that he had put another big box there to keep me trapped. I gently shut the door and went back to the bed.

The next day, August 14th, he came into the dungeon with his shotgun. I knew he was livid and braced myself for his violence. He never pointed the gun at me, but used it as a wand of power against me. He threatened me, "If you ever tell anyone anything, I will kill you! The police better not come back!" I said nothing in fear of being killed. Then without another word being said, he turned and left the room.

The next few days went by slowly as I felt that there was no hope for my future. Again, he quickly took control of me and had me trapped in fear of him. I knew I needed to get away from him, but how?

Early in the morning on August 23, the door was opened for me. This was the last straw. I was in the dungeon watching television and suddenly the door was kicked in. It scared me to death, more than the time the Constable burst in on me. He charged towards me cursing and mumbling. He demanded to me, "I want your money. Give it to me now!" My purse was on the bed next to me and he grabbed it. Somehow the strap became entangled around my neck as he pulled it and me off the bed. The purse strap broke and I fell to the ground. It happened so fast, I guess I panicked and tried to hold onto my purse. He started kicking and hitting me as I tried to get up. I managed to climb to my feet just to be hit in the face with his fist. This knocked me back into the TV and it fell to the ground and broke. I fell onto three boxes of my things that had been packed up and could hear many things breaking with me on top of them. He grabbed my purse and ran into the living room and tore it to pieces looking for the money, but it was not there. I had hidden it in my pillowcase.

Several minutes later, he returned and seemed to be a different person. He said in a calm voice, "I want to work things out and fix our marriage."

His actions had me confused and I said, "Ok, Please leave me alone." I fell asleep only to be awaked by a soft female voice in my left ear. It whispered, "GET OUT! SAVE YOUR LIFE!" Immediately, I jumped up and knew it was God speaking directly to me. It was now or never. I was either going to jump without a net and save my life, or I was going to die! For the first time in my marriage, I listened to my faith. I opened the door with fear and hope and said to him, "If you want to fix our marriage, I need to go to church."

He said, "You can go tomorrow." That night I was too excited to sleep as I had managed to get him to open the door for me to run! I knew that it was now or never because God had told me it was time for me to run.

Chapter 13
Getting Out!

I waited in the dungeon until he fell asleep. Around 11 a.m., I snuck out of the house with my ID and one hundred dollars. I decided not to take my car, as he would know that I was gone. I walked as fast as I could to UMC Quickcare on Rancho Blvd. When I walked in, I told the receptionist what I was, a battered and abused wife! It was liberating for me to finally be able to tell someone what he had done to me. Almost instantly I felt a huge weight lift off my shoulders. It felt as though I was a new person!

They quickly took me back into an examination room. When the doctor came in to see me, I was kind of relieved that it was a woman. After a quick look over, she started asking me questions and filling out papers for Domestic Violence. Then they took pictures of my many bruises that covered my face and body. As she left the room, she told me, "It's going to be ok. I'm going to call it in." I assumed that they were calling the police. Several minutes passed and they came back and told me I could go home. When I informed them that I had walked there, they offered to call me a cab and I accepted. I thought that when I arrived at home, he would be gone. I assumed that the police would have already picked him up.

A big mistake was made. They had NOT called it in and I walked back into a dangerous situation. As I opened the door and saw him still there, my heart stopped, total terror ran through my body. Luckily for me, he was still passed out when I came back in. He had no idea that I had left or that anything out of the ordinary was going on.

I thought for sure that I would be returning home to a safe environment for once, but it was more dangerous than ever before since I had told the outside world about his abuse towards me. However, I was put right back into my personal hell. I quietly walked back into the dungeon and climbed into the bed. Not knowing who I would be dealing with when he woke up terrified me.

With a sharpie marker, I wrote on the outside of the bedroom door begging him to leave me alone! As I look at the picture now, I can see my Post Traumatic Stress Syndrome or the drugs he was giving me were taking a toll on my mental ability. Some of my writings don't make sense. I wrote such things as my address and how I was feeling. I think it was also a way for me to tell my story if he killed me.

I wrote exactly how I was feeling and the way he was treating me since the Police left. I told him that he didn't understand anything I was trying to say or how I felt both physically and mentally. Even though I didn't anymore, I wrote "I Love You" several times because he always made me say it. I put it there in hope that he wouldn't barge in and harass me. It was also a way to keep him from getting angry and hurting me again. And of course I had to include his favorite quotes, "I forgot" and "I'm sorry." In the picture, the box that he used to pin me into the dungeon is right there in the foreground.

I was lying there wondering what had happened, why had the system failed me? They couldn't have wanted me to go back to a dangerous situation. Thinking to myself, I wondered what I should do now. I had already started the ball rolling and couldn't allow it to stop!

When he woke up, he immediately started bothering me. He ignored the writing on the door. I think he sensed something was different with me this time around. He was in a calm state for now and kept pushing me to agree to work our marriage out and fix things between us. He was promising to never hit me again. But I knew it was just the same old crap coming out of his mouth. It would be like every other time I let it slide, good for a day or two and then right back to the monster that he was. Our marriage was over in my heart and now my mind was in agreement, it was over! No longer was I going to be a prisoner of his, a punching bag, or someone he could lie to every word he spoke to me! This time I was finally going to take the hand that God had tried to reach out for me several times before. Now was the time for me to GET OUT!

I knew that when Steven and I met, my heart had the right intent, to be loved unconditionally forever. However, I was deceived and was led down the wrong path. I chose to stay on that path for far too long. The decision I was about to make was going to impact me and change my life forever. Enough was enough. There was no turning back. I was going to get out and survive this and never look back.

I didn't have much time to plan for my escape. It was something I should have thought about and prepared for long ago. But the ball was rolling and I had no intention of stopping it. I knew that I had to jump without a net and just go for it and save my life.

The next few days, he continued asking me to work things out between us. I knew it was over, but needed to buy myself some time to prepare. While hiding in the dungeon, I quickly began to think about my next move. Realizing that I would have no money because he was the one with the job, I called to him, "Can you come here?" He walked into the room and before he could say a word, I told him, "If you want to fix our marriage, you need to go to the store for me."

He asked me, "What do you want me to get you?"

"Go to the grocery store and call me and I will tell you want I want you to get," I said to him with a smile. He turned and left the house and called me a few minutes later from the store.

"I'm here," he said.

I told him what I wanted him to buy, toothbrushes, toothpaste, toilet paper, ect. I had him buy me enough essentials to last me about six months. To my amazement, he bought everything I asked for. When he asked me why he was buying all this stuff, I told him, "I just want to stock up for an emergency." He seemed confused, but he did it anyway.

When he returned home and put everything away, I informed him that he had to make the living room look like a living room again. He had been using it as his bedroom and I wanted it to look better. I said, "You need to move your things into the den so that the living room will look normal." Again he did what I asked without question. I must have caught him on a good day, which were very rare. When he finished with the living room, my final request for him was to hang the flag over the garage. I don't know why I made him do that, but it seemed fun to be the boss.

A week prior to this, I made an appointment with and attorney, Matthew Harter, ESQ. knowing that I would be able to get out of the house with the excuse that I was going to church. When I left the dungeon to go to the lawyer, I took all the money I had saved in my pillowcase, almost ten thousand dollars. He asked me, "Where do you think you are going?"

I responded, "You said I could go to church."

With that, he turned his head away from me and said, "Ok." I calmly walked out the front door and left. I couldn't believe that he didn't question me about it because it was the middle of the day on Tuesday. I was scared that he would have turned violent when I tried to leave but thankfully he didn't. I guess he really wanted to fix our marriage, but I could no longer be abused and knew it was only a matter of time before he snapped again. I was not worried that he might want to come with me, because in the eighteen years we were married, he only went to church with me once and it was like pulling teeth to get him to go.

When I met with the lawyer, I told him everything. He took $4000.00 as a retainer. I assumed that would pay for my divorce, but I was wrong. I learned a lot about what I should have done the hard way and this became another horrible thing for me. What I should've done was contact a shelter for victims of domestic violence and had them help me. Unfortunately, I thought the system failed me and I was on my own. But there were many people out there waiting to help me if I would've asked, or known who to ask for help. There are a lot of people that are more than willing to help victims get out of the mess they are in. All we have to do is ask! A shelter would've helped me find a lawyer to take me case Pro-Bono.

My attorney advised me to get a protective order against Steven so that he would have to leave me alone. He told me what I had to do. I needed to go to the Family Court. At Family Court, it really hit me hard, the fact that I WAS a victim of a violent crime. You are given a serial number. They bring you into the back and take pictures of all of your cuts and bruises. They took about twenty-five pictures of me.

I was granted a Protective Order immediately. Steven was to stay 1000 yards from our residence and me. He was not supposed to go anywhere that I would go, for which was not many places since I was a prisoner in my own home. He was also not allowed to call me or own a firearm. With him loving his guns, I knew that this might be a big problem.

Upon returning home, I felt empowered. The foundation was laid for me to GET OUT! I had really done it. I couldn't believe it; I was almost free of his abuses forever. I went into the dungeon, which seemed to be brighter with my newfound security. I hid the divorce papers and the Protective Order between the mattresses. Waiting for the right time to have him served. I didn't know when it would be, but knew that it wouldn't be long.

On September 16, 2005, I opened the dungeon door to try to get something to eat. He had put a big box in front of the door to block me in. My foot caught the box as I stepped over it and I fell into the wall. I continued down the hall and he had put a big basket with a black trash bag in it full of something that would make it too heavy for me to move. Again, I stepped over it, but this time I fell to the ground. He said, "What the fuck are you doing?" as he climbed off the couch and headed towards me.

As he approached me, I told him, "Please don't touch me, I'll go back into the room." He moved the basket and the box for me to walk past them and back into the room.

The next day around 10 p.m., I took a long hot shower and imagined my old life being washed away. After my cleansing, I went into the living room and headed towards the kitchen. I tripped over the black cord he had across the floor. He tried to help me get up, but I was hurt and pissed off that the cord was still there. He said, "Are you alright?"

Angry, I said, "NO! Please don't touch me!"

He responded, "I don't know what your problem is."

Without saying a word, I rose to my feet and went back into the bedroom and closed the door behind me, knowing that I made the right decision about the divorce. Nothing could be worse than staying with a man that doesn't love you and treats you as his property. If he wanted to fix our marriage, he would have removed that cord from the floor.

Pain

I feel this Pain
Piercing every fiber of my being
Tears cascading down like waterfalls
Is there really no way of escaping this?
It's harder now than ever
There is no drug
There is nothing to hide behind
I'm so exposed to this pain
Face to face
Most of my life I've known this pain
I've been running forever
Suddenly I find
I'm not in the race
I'm not running
I am still
I am stoic
I'm realizing not much has changed
Just how to deal with it
Now I must make some sense out of this
Do I continue in the cycle of deceit?
Do I allow myself to be humiliated?
To be unappreciated?
Or am I finally to see
What I've chosen not to see for years
To be real
To be real is to be mature
I'm going to be mature this time
I may not like the path I am to take
But I must stop this madness
I deserve better
I can't give anymore than I have given
I have opened myself up again
Just to be slammed into this Pain again!

About an hour later, when my body stopped hurting from my fall, I walked into the living room and said something to him about the cord. I don't remember what I said or the tone in which I said it. He yelled, "Shut the fuck up!" When he said that, my heart started beating really fast and I began to shake. He was changing back into the monster. He snapped and began yelling and cursing at me very loudly. Not wanting to be abused again, I went back into the bedroom and dialed 911. The 911 operators could hear what was going on and everything he was yelling. I told her, "I'm scared!"

She told me, "Stay in the room and don't hang up the phone. Help is on the way." She continued to listen to his tirade while assuring me that help was almost there. Within a few short minutes, the doorbell rang.

When the police arrived, Steven was shocked. He tried acting like nothing was wrong. I stayed in the bedroom listening and heard him tell the police that he had the flu. I thanked the 911 Operator and hung up. Seconds later, there was a gentle knock on my bedroom door. I opened it to see a female police officer standing there. She came into the room and asked me if I was ok. I said with a smile, "I am now." I handed her the divorce papers along with the Protective Order and asked if she would give them to him. She smiled as she reached out her hand to take them and said, "Absolutely". Steven turned ten shades of white when he received the papers. He said, "I thought we were working it out? You're a double cross."

In a way, I did double cross him, but I had no choice. He would never have allowed me to do any of this had he known what I was up to. One of the officers told him, "Get some clothes and shampoo because you're not coming back."

I told the officers about his guns and even the one he had in his car. They went to his car and removed it from his possession. The female officer followed me into the bedroom to remove the gun he had in there. The officers told him that he had to leave the property and not return. He was not arrested because he didn't hit me this time and the charges I pressed at Family Court were not filed yet. All they were able to do was make him leave.

After they left, I was in a bit of shock. It was almost unbelievable that I was free. I should've been scared to be in the house alone, but for some reason I wasn't. It was like I had just done something miraculous, an emotional high is probably the best way to describe how I was feeling. I was proud of myself for sticking to my guns and going through with what should've been done years earlier.

I know the scared little girl is still there inside of me. It's up to me now to show myself how much I care. Through my little girl eyes, I saw and suffered so much at the hands of an abusive father. I had no idea how the damage I sustained in my childhood would affect me in my adult life. I grew up too fast and all alone. Paying a great price along the way. The feelings of loss and abandonment have plagued me and taken their toll with much regret and wasted life. Aloneness, I know that well. I have felt alone my entire life. The only presence I have felt with me is that of Jesus. My faith has never failed me. Even now that I'm on the ground and broken, I know someday, someway Jesus will save the day. As I pray, I pray for a brighter tomorrow with laughter and guidance and no more sorrow. Leaving an abusive marriage and starting over is the hardest task I've yet to take on. I spent 18 years with a carbon copy of my father. Now that I have broken away and ended the abuse in my life, I am so alone. I have no family, no children, nothing but my faith and hope that there is a better life out there for me. One that I never could have imagined, one with a loving family and a safe place to call home.

Throughout the night I kept thanking God and Jesus for their love, guidance, strength and protection. Steven had kept me in a fog; I wasn't able to think straight and somehow was able to GET OUT! and get help. It had been months since I had last driven a car or even left the house except for doctor's appointments. I was given the strength to stand my ground and keep to the plan and save my life. I was very proud of myself for not caving in to the fear and gaining my freedom and life back. All of my life, I knew that God and Jesus were watching over me and protecting me from him even though I was blind to their sign to GET OUT! And save my life.

Free Yourself!

Jesus, I prayed
Please save my life
Had a man, he called me his wife
Thank God Above
That evil man
Did not take my life
He hit me once
He hit me twice
He hit me many times in my life
I've paid the price
He looked in my blue-green eyes
And lied and lied
He yelled out loud
And wished I would die
Jesus the Christ, I cried
Please save my life
Cried my eyes out
Blue-green eyes, blue-green eyes
They mesmerize
Jesus, I cried
I'm a teller of the truth
I have a message for your children
We are all brothers and sisters
We all bleed red blood
Sacrifice to Christ
Jesus, Please grant me
A chance at life
Break the cycle
Free yourself!

The first night alone, I couldn't sleep. The emotional high I was feeling was incredible. It almost felt like I was a new woman. I explored the house and went into rooms that he had kept me out of. As my journey around the house continued, I kept finding signs that I had done the right thing. They were very reassuring to me. I started finding cigarettes hidden everywhere. It's amazing how it went on right under my nose and he had the nerve to lie about it. I found pornography on the computer and DVD's in the den. I also began to find more loaded guns that he had hidden that I didn't know he had. But the most startling thing I found was a life insurance policy that he had taken out on me without my knowledge. It was set up like I took it out and named him as beneficiary. As I looked it over, it stated that if I die, he would receive $350,000.00. I believe without a doubt that he had plans for me. The next day I called the insurance company and let them know he forged my name and told them to void the policy.

All through the night, not once did I stop to think what my future would be like or how I was going to make ends meet. It didn't bother me. The only thing on my mind was that I was free.

The normal life that my heart yearned for was finally at hand. I could now do what ever I wanted. I always tried to be a good person and help other people. Being trapped with Steven, it limited me in every way. With me wanting to go to church and him wanting no part of it made that simple pleasure for me impossible. Without him to stop me, now it was my time and I was going to grab a hold and not let go.

Most of the night I just enjoyed the tranquility all around me. It had been a long time since there was this much peace and quiet. I was finally able to hear myself think and not be bothered by him every ten minutes.

At about 4 a.m. the phone rang. It only rang once, but I knew it had to be Steven. He was violating the protective order by calling, which is probably why he hung up after one ring. It did startle me, but my determination not to be his prisoner again gave me the power to resist.

My faith gave me the strength and without it, there was no way I could've or would've been able to GET OUT!

Just after 8 a.m., the phone rang again. This time I was able to answer it. It was his mother, Harriet. It was no surprise to me that she called, it was expected. She needed to be in control of Steven ever since I met him. She didn't ask me what had happened. She quickly jumped into telling me, more like ordering me to drop the protective order and let him come back. She told me, "It's not fair that he had to leave the house."

Responding, I told her, "He had been very abusive to me both physically and verbally. I have suffered by his hand far too long."

She cut in, "That's something we can deal with later!"

Instantly, I realized that she didn't care about what he had been doing to me. All she cared about was her son. She continued to bark at me, but I had faith on my side and didn't falter.

"We can work something out, but only if you drop the protective order," she said. She had no control of the situation and was getting frustrated.

I told her, "The one thing that I will not do is drop the protective order or the domestic violence charges."

In a snotty tone, she said, "If you don't drop the charges, he will not give you any money and your life will be hell."

"My life has already been hell and it cannot get any worse," I told her.

It's too bad for her that I wasn't concerned about money. I was concerned about saving my life before he took it and my life with him had already been hell! I stood my ground as she kept trying to talk me into letting him come back. Knowing that this call was getting me nowhere and remembering that my attorney advised me not to talk to her, I hung up the phone. At that moment I made a decision not to talk to her again. She continued to call several more times, but I just let the phone ring. It kind of made me feel empowered.

If I'd let him come back, he would've probably killed me for going behind his back to get the protective order and divorce papers. The only way I was able to GET OUT! was to not allow him to know what I was doing and not leave any clues about my plans.

The morning after he was removed, I was introduced to two Victims Advocates from the Police Department. Their names were Rebecca and Jan. Both of them had been Domestic Violence Police Advocates for many years. They became my support as I had no friends to lean on and no one to talk to. They were always there when ever I needed them. I call them my angels for helping me. They went over and above what was required of them. They really care for the people they help. They also made arrangements for me to see a doctor. For their support, I must thank them. Thank You, both! When they came into the house, they were appalled and told me that it had an eerie feeling. They saw the black cord across the floor and the writing on the door. They told me that they had seen many horrible cases and my case was the worst that they had ever seen.

Steven had no choice but to retain legal counsel. He denied ever hitting me or being abusive in any way. However, the hospital visits and doctor's records would prove him wrong. Even though I never stated at the time that it was abuse, the facts were there. He tried to contest the divorce and was determined not to give me a cent. After eighteen years of marriage, I was entitled to half. I didn't want anymore than what I was entitled to.

Chapter 14
On My Own

Standing my ground and holding on to my new freedom amazed me. I never believed enough in myself to think that I could ever break away from him and regain my identity and self-esteem. I certainly didn't know my own strength; I had no idea how mentally strong I really was. Knowing that it would be hard on my own, I knew it would be worth whatever I had to go through to make it. If I stayed in that marriage, I would have become a statistic. I had to be a survivor and tell my story to help save other people from going through the hell I lived for far too long.

I didn't stay with him because I loved him. I stayed with him because I was stuck with him. I was not strong enough to keep him from taking my identity and self-esteem. He commanded control of everything, our finances, friends, and every other aspect of our lives. It felt like I was his property and not his wife. I had no say in any matter that concerned us. I was not listed on our bank accounts or credit cards. I was forced to rely on him for everything. Sometimes it felt like I was in quicksand, the more I tried to get some control, the more control he took.

With my faith on my side, I knew that I would make it on my own. It would not be easy without him, but I knew that I could make a better life for myself, a life where I had my own identity and was free to be safe and happy. My strong faith kept me believing that I could turn something tragic into something positive.

It was not an easy thing to do, I had no idea how hard my life would soon become. I had to relearn everything for myself and become an independent person again. However, I also had no idea how many wonderful people and things would come my way.

The first few days on my own were wonderful. My body was able to clean out whatever it was he had me on and my thoughts were clearing. I was now able to get a solid eight hours sleep without him coming in to bother me. I couldn't remember the last time I felt rested. For the first time in over a year, I was able to eat something other than a frozen macaroni and cheese.

Being on my own, I knew it was up to me to get myself back together and figure out what was physically wrong with me. I began to contact all the doctors I had seen in recent years to get a hold of my medical records; with all my records in one place someone should be able to help me. When I called Universal Medical Center records department, the person on the other end of the line told me, "I hear a weakness in your voice like your spirit has died." When he said that, it lit something up inside of me, a feeling that someone might understand what I had been through. He was very kind and compassionate to me. He asked, "Are you OK?"

I replied, "No, not really." With that we began talking and struck up a friendship. His name was Shaun, it turned out that he was fifteen years younger than I was. He was twenty-five and I was forty. We had a lot in common, especially the meda physical world. We talked on the phone for hours and the conversation never seemed to go dry.

After talking for almost a week, we decided to meet. When we met, there was a strong physical attraction between us. It was a great feeling for me as Steven constantly told me that I was not attractive and lucky to have him! Here was this younger man that had an interest in me. Going against what I thought was right or wrong, we began dating and soon developed a physical relationship. I felt it was right, because I needed to feel alive again, and wrong because it had only been a few days since I had Steven removed from my life.

It had been several years since I had been touched or held in a loving manner. Shaun was good for me. He lit a fire back up inside of me and helped me regain my self-confidence. He made me feel beautiful and sexy again, a feeling that I had not had in about fifteen years. We were like best friends, so the age difference was not an issue for either of us. Understanding my situation with my life, he didn't push me too hard. He knew that I had no money and he would bring food over for me to eat. We would watch funny movies that he would bring over to make me laugh. He taught me how to live and laugh again, something that I really needed at this point in my life.

Our physical relationship lasted about two months before I realized it wasn't right. Explaining to him that I had strong feelings for him, we could not be together because I fell for him in a time of weakness. It was a time when I needed him emotionally and physically. I wanted to be friends with him and not lovers. Never meaning to hurt him, unfortunately I did. I often felt bad for hurting him, but I knew what was supposed to be. We remained friends, even though I knew that he was hoping for one day to get back together with me. I feel that God had brought him into my life at a time when I needed someone to help me come out of my shell and the person that God brought to me was Shaun.

I was always worried that Steven would try to come after me. Around 4 a.m. one night I heard noises outside the house. I turned on the light and called 911. When the police arrived, they checked the area where I heard the noises. By the doggie door, they found Steven's glasses, cigarettes and a loaded gun clip. He was soon arrested for violating the protective order. It was an ordeal that I was expecting to happen and knew would probably happen again.

My neighbors, Scott and Cindy would come over several times a week and we would talk about God and Jesus. It was uplifting to me to have someone that I could talk to about faith, as I had not yet found a church that felt right to me. I was invited to attend their Mormon church and I accepted, but after attending I knew it was not for me. They also understood my situation and would bring food with them to help me get by. They were very nice people and I appreciated their time and generosity. Some of the neighborhood kids would mow the lawn for me. It was very nice, as I had no money to pay them.

There were many nice people around me. My disability attorney's office gave me $100 for food. My victim's advocates gave me presents from the Secret Santa fund. Several of my neighbor's came forward and provided help to me. There is help out there for the asking, my mistake was not opening my eyes to see it sooner.

I continued to search for a church to help keep my faith strong. Not far from my house, I saw a huge building that turned out to be a Christian Church. It was just after hurricane Katrina. As I went in and talked to some people there, it seemed like a good church. I found a seat and the service began. About half way through the sermon, the pastor began asking for people to donate to the victims of the hurricane. I thought to myself this is good, until the pastor said, "I want to raise enough money to buy a jet and fly to New Orleans and help the people there." I quickly had a bad feeling about this place. I thought why did he need to buy a jet and fly there and help them? The money he would spend on a jet could have really helped a lot of people there.

After the service was over, I was brought back to meet the pastor and he seemed to look upon his congregation as being below him. It was not what I was looking for in a church and never returned there.

At family court, Steven was very bitter towards me, he tried to fight everything. He was going to make things as hard for me as he could. It was stressful, but worth every bit for me to get my life back. Arrangements were made for him to get his things.

At court, we agreed that he could come to the house at 3 p.m. to get his things. I was nervous, as I had nobody to be there with me. To my surprise and relief, he never showed up. I began to let my guard down and relax.

Around 4:30, while I was relaxed, there was a loud banging on the door. It startled me and I jumped from my chair. "Open the door! Tami," Steven yelled in a very demanding voice. With the tone of his voice, I wasn't sure about his state of mind. He was more than an hour late and I didn't know if he was drunk or high. I feared for my safety and thought he might come after me. I called the police and they came and arrested him. I felt bad that he was arrested, but he always played by his own rules. Not this time, he was going to play by the rules of the court. We agreed on 3 p.m. not 4 p.m.

After that, arrangements were made for movers to come pack up his belongings. I told the movers to take all of his things because I needed to start over and didn't want to hold onto anything of his. The movers left some of his tools and car parts in the garage because there wasn't enough room in the truck. A towing company came and towed his 1969 Chevrolet Nova that he rebuilt with our money.

After his stuff was taken, he claimed that he didn't get his tools back. He took me back to court over the issue of his tools several times and wasted thousands of dollars that I would have to pay in attorney's fees. It was a way for him to continue to hurt me, as he knew that I had no money. Everything that was left was moved into a storage unit and I paid it for three months. My attorney informed his attorney about their whereabouts and gave him the key. He went to the storage unit and took what he wanted and left the rest, which was later sold by the storage company.

With me having no money, I couldn't afford to buy food for me, yet alone our dogs. A time was set up for him to come get them. This time he showed up right on time. I opened to door and the dogs ran to his car and jumped in. He then drove off and I never saw the dogs again. I asked my attorney to find out about them and he told me to move on. To this day, I wonder about them. For a while, their love was the only love I received.

In court, I was surprised that the female judge didn't show any compassion towards me. Steven was getting away with lying to the court and playing games with them and me. This process was mentally draining on me and was causing me to lose weight. The weight loss made me happy, but emotionally I needed something.

Talking to my nephew Robert one day on the phone, he told me about his friend Jack Sharky. Jack had overcome things in his own life with his faith. Robert asked me if I would like to talk to Jack and I said, "Yes."

Jack soon called me and talked to me about his church. His church was Mountain View Christian Church at 3900 E. Bonanza Road in Las Vegas, Nevada. He told me about how down to earth the pastor was, how great the congregation was, and how powerful and uplifting the music was. He also told me many wonderful stories of how lives were being changed for the better there. He told me I would be welcomed there. It made me feel good, however I was still not sure.

The following Sunday, Jack called me from church and let me listen to the music and it gave me a warm, welcoming feeling inside. I knew I needed to go to this church as I felt it calling me. Jack would call me often and read scripture to me, which helped me keep my faith strong and he always seemed to know the right scripture to read to me. I believe that God sent Jack to keep my faith strong. I am very grateful to Jack for what he did for me. I really wanted to attend his church and see what it was like for myself.

Finally one Sunday, I went to Mountain View Christian Church. On the way in, I looked up at the cross and instantly felt my spirit come alive again. When I first walked in, I received a warm feeling run through my body, it felt like a kiss from God. People in the lobby were friendly and welcomed me. As I found a seat, the band started playing music and I felt like I was home. The sound of the music and the holy voices singing wonderful songs ignited my faith and I couldn't help myself from joining in with the music. It was made easy because they had screens on the walls with the words written to help me sing along.

Then the pastor came onto the stage, his name is Pastor Tom Van Kempen. As I listened to his sermon, I could sense that he was a real person and he didn't look down onto his congregation, he was a part of it. He understood life's situations and could reference them to the Bible, which is what I had been looking for in a church for a long time. After church ended, I was convinced that I had finally found the right church for me. I was so excited. I wanted to tell everyone about it.

Every Sunday I would go to church, not having any money, my Mother would give me money for gas so I could go to church. Jack's wife, Maria bought me a divorce care book at church to help me get through the divorce. This church really cares about its congregation and they show it. Later, I was able to pay her back for the booklet that was very helpful to me.

Two months after Steven was removed from the house, I still had not received any money from him. Needing help financially and emotionally, I went to a shelter in Las Vegas for victims of domestic violence called Safe Nest. I should have contacted them sooner as they could've helped me and provided resources that I needed. They offer a safe place to stay, food, counseling and even help with lawyers that work pro-bono and job placement.

The staff at Safe Nest felt that because of my trauma and post-traumatic stress syndrome that it would be best for me to have my own room and not be surrounded by crying babies. There was a single room available, but it was on the second floor and with my herniated disc in my back, I was a liability for them and therefore they couldn't do much to help me at that time. So, I had to stay in the house even though it was dangerous and I had no money. My victim's advocates, Jan and Rebecca, through a state fund helped me pay the power and water bills and change the locks on the doors.

Back in Family Court, the issue of the house was brought up. With me being unable to pay the mortgage and Steven unwilling to pay it, the court ordered it to be sold. Two realtors were assigned to sell the house. A month later, we still had no luck selling. In the mail, someone had sent me a big folded picture of Jesus made out of cloth. To this day, I do not know who sent it to me. The instructions read, "This cloth is for you to ask Jesus for what you need. After you ask for what you need, fold it up and return it in the return envelop." I took the picture to my alter in the living room, lit a candle and spread the picture out on the floor and knelt in front of it. Putting my hands on the cloth, I prayed to Jesus, "Please help me sell my house and get $25,000 so that I can pay my attorney's fees and move." Blowing out the candle after I finished my prayer, I gently folded up the picture and put it back in the mail.

The very next day, my doorbell rang. It was the sister-in-law of my neighbor. She said, "I am interested in buying your house. Can I come in and look at it?" I invited her in to have a look around. She loved the house and wanted to buy it. I was very happy and relieved that Jesus answered my prayer. I was so thankful that I kept saying thank you to Jesus and God.

In late November 2005, I met a man named John. He was about my age and I found him to be attractive, but I was not really interested in a relationship with him. He had just retired from the Marines. Six months earlier, he returned from Iraq. He suffered from post-traumatic stress syndrome also, so we had a connection. He was recently divorced and had no children. John was my protection from Steven. My neighbor's saw Steven driving by the house on a regular basis, sometimes parking down the street to watch me. The police were called and he was arrested again for violating the protective order. I was always on edge in that house, every noise I heard scared me thinking that it was him coming back to get me. He was a very sneaky and unpredictable person, I feared for my life with him out there somewhere.

Chapter 15
Rebuilding My Life

With the house being sold, I began to pack up. I was getting stronger everyday, mentally and physically. Most of my strength was found in my faith and by going to Mountain View Christian Church. Whenever I was in church, I could feel Jesus with me there. Through Pastor Tom's sermons, I could see that God was working on my life and helping me by teaching and preparing me for life without Steven.

Having no money made me do things I never thought I would need to do. I was now relying on other people to get food and pay bills. I spent Thanksgiving looking for a job. My old boss from Canyon Ranch, Jean was now working at the Spa at the Aladdin Hotel and Casino. She gave me hope, I didn't know if I would be able to do nails anymore because of my back and the hives. But having no choice, I gave it a try. I needed a job so that I could start to take care of myself. One my first day of work, the Las Vegas Marathon was going on. It was difficult getting to work, but I was happy to be going through it for the rewards of getting back on my feet.

The first four days working were not very busy. My back hurt, but it was manageable. The fifth day was crazy busy and about half way through it; my back began to spasm and pain was shooting down my legs. I continued to work with the pain, but knew that I could no longer do nails. I was disappointed. I was hoping to land on my feet and be able to take care of myself. At the end of the day, I told Jean, "Thank you for giving me a chance, but my body is in too bad of shape to continue to work. I didn't know what I was going to do. I just put it in God's hands.

With my half of the proceeds from selling the house, which was just what I asked Jesus for, I moved into an apartment on the other side of town. It was the first time I had ever lived on my own. I didn't want to live anywhere around Steven and all of the memories. My attorney told me that I owed him $10,000 on top of the $4,000 I had already paid him. Then after I paid him, he told me that he could no longer represent me in my divorce. I paid him $14,000 and had nothing to show for it, I was still married to Steven. I had to start all over again, I felt very dejected and confused. If I had gone through the system, an attorney would have taken my case pro-bono and saved me time, stress and money.

I was excited and scared at the same time. I felt that moving far away from Steven and the memories of our marriage would be good for me to move on. I signed a one-year lease in an apartment on the other side of town, which I thought would be plenty of time for me to find a job and get on with my life.

Upon moving into my apartment, I began looking for a job. It was harder than I expected and I kept coming up empty. Still I kept trying, as I knew that eventually I would find something. I was learning how to live again, paying my bills and taking care of myself. I was just learning things I should've already known.

Steven continued to burn through my money by dragging me back to court. I knew that I needed to find another attorney. I found an attorney that agreed to help me after hearing about my last attorney. His name is William Potter. I couldn't believe that the Judge was tolerating Steven's foolish games with the court. He was defying everything that the court ordered him to do.

I think him taking me back to court was his way of wearing me down to the point that I might go back to him. My resolve was strong and with my faith guiding me, I was able to resist his games and continue to be free and safe. Steven was ordered to pay me half of our 401k, but I never received any money from him. With my divorce final, I still feared Steven and took precautions to protect myself. My divorce was finalized on June 2, 2006 and Mr. Potter didn't charge me anything.

Mr. Potter was elected Family Court Judge right before finalizing my divorce. He is a good man and I wish him the best.

One day, I was down to my last $20. I took it to the Casino down the road and found a video poker machine. I prayed for help as I inserted it into the machine. God answered my prayer and delivered me a jackpot. It was enough money to get me through a few months. It was something I did out of desperation and I do not recommend it to anyone.

Throughout my court ordeal, I would get comfort from church. I went to church on a regular basis, when things were good and bad. Although I expected things to happen right away for me, they did not. I believe God wanted me to prove my faith. Times were hard for me. I spent Thanksgiving and Christmas alone. On Christmas Eve, I went to church alone and had no Christmas dinner.

I found a few friends. One of my friends was very spiritual. She would talk to me on the phone for hours. She would pray for me and she told me that there was going to be a miracle in my life. She said, "Jesus is watching over you and so was the blessed Mother Mary." She also said that I was going to find true love with the one that was made for me. I focused on that and prayed he would find me.

I did finally get a job. It was at Wal-Mart. It was hard for me as my back injury made it difficult to stand for 8 hours. But needing to support myself, I continued to work there.

My faith was getting stronger and going to church lifted my spirit. There were times I had $5 to my name and would go to church and put it in the tithing basket. My faith was strong and I knew in my heart that God and Jesus were not going to abandon me. I kept believing in my faith. There is a reason prayers are not answered right away. It takes time for us to learn what God is trying to teach us and then our prayers can be answered. I continued going to church and held my faith close to my heart. Pastor Tom's wife Robin prayed over me. She prayed that I would be healed of my pain and that I would find a job and happiness. There were many people at church that prayed for me and I want to thank every one of them.

On Feb. 19, 2006, I was water baptized at Mountain View Christian Church. It was a wonderful feeling. I put my life completely in God's hands. I knew it was only a matter of time before I would be on my feet again.

Going to church continued to be a staple in my life. I needed to hear the music to lift my spirit and Pastor Tom's sermons guided me. It seemed that every sermon was written just for me. Sitting there listening to him preach was a powerful and wonderful experience for me. God brings people into your life when you need them, you just need to open your eyes and see what they are there to do. Jack brought me to church. Pastor Tom guided me towards healing and not giving up. He helped me embrace life without Stephen.

Sometimes I would get sad at church. I would look around at the congregation and men and women together, some with their children. I would be very envious of them and wonder if they knew just how lucky they really were. I would sit there and wish that I had someone that loved me and would go to church with me. I became so lonely at times; I would just sit in my room and cry. I was not prepared for most of what I had to do to be on my own, especially the loneliness. I really wanted to be loved by the right man. Meeting men was not a problem, but the right one was not in sight.

There were times I wondered if I had made the right choice. Times were different and jobs were not just waiting to be found. My disabilities made my search more difficult as I was limited to what I could do. I was not prepared for it to be difficult to find work that would pay enough to support myself. I honestly had no idea of how I would make it on my own.

My constant was my faith and my church. I continued to attend church every Wednesday night and Sunday mornings. I was diligent about my commitment to Christ. My faith was what gave me strength and defined me. At times I felt like I was in the dark with no way out. I couldn't see anything, but a voice from within and my heart full of Gods love kept me going. Sometimes I just cried out to God for help and to heal my soul. I continued to believe in my faith when I couldn't see what was a head for me!

I understood that I had to re-discover myself. I was frozen in time for so long, I forgot who I was. Steven took my identity, hopes and dreams. It was now time for me to breathe life back into them. I spent a year on my own to find myself again. Writing songs and poems about my life helped me understand my life and what had happened to me. Listening to music lightened up my spirit. I also watched a Christian artist Jeremy Camp. His music talked to me and inspired me. I bought a DVD of him and watched it repeatedly.

During the year on my own, I went to counseling at Harmony Health Care. I saw Dr. David and he really helped me. He explained to me that what had happened to me was not my fault. I was a victim! My life and mental state were fractured from the trauma of my old life. He taught me new techniques to apply to my life that would guide me and prevent me from ever allowing anyone to ever cross the line again. I learned that I had a voice! He also taught me how to communicate in the real world.

He also informed me that I had started laying a new foundation and setting boundary lines the minute I had Steven served with the divorce papers and protective order. I learned how to say "Enough" and "No". Most importantly, I realized that I had broken the cycle of violence and abuse not only in my life but the vicious cycle that plagued my family. With the chain now broken, I could begin the process of freeing myself. Looking back on it, I was impatient. I wanted a quick fix, but that was impossible. Dr. David told me that 18 years of marriage to an abusive man could take a lifetime to repair. And that was if I was able to come out of it and regain myself and understand fully that I was the victim. Victim's of Violent Crimes through the State of Nevada provided some more counseling and help.

My heart was starving for love. In my total aloneness, I realized that before I could ever go down the road to a relationship with someone else that I first needed to love myself. I knew that God wouldn't bring someone into my life before I was ready to handle a relationship. I was not ready or deserving of him in my current state.

In my healing first came my love for Jesus and God. Then with a lot of soul searching, an unconditional love for myself began to emerge. As a disabled woman with severe Post-Traumatic Stress Syndrome and extreme physical pain, I accepted myself for who I was and not what I was. I realized that I had a hunger for life and it was an incredible feeling of joy.

Being 18 years older now, I no longer relied on my looks to help me. I began to see the beauty within me. My glow was undeniable and getting brighter every day. When you love yourself and God, you have a glow. It's called an aura.

The entire year on my own, I continued to work on myself. When I would stumble or fall I would get back up. I kept myself surrounded in a total positive mode. I call it PMA, Positive Mental Attitude. It works, it did for me and it can for everybody. Before I would say "I can't". Now I say "I can!" When a negative came, I kicked it out and replaced it with a positive. I continued to raise the bar for myself with baby steps. I needed to learn how to walk before I could run!

In my desperation for financial survival, I went to a program at Help of Southern Nevada. They offered a program for displaced housewives. This course really helped me. The class taught us how to give a good interview and how to prepare for it. They also sent me on a job interview with the MGM Hotel and Casino.

While waiting to hear back from the MGM, I was invited to by the Job Coordinator to appear on his radio show. The show was called "Native Calls". On the show, we talked about my abuse. People were allowed to call in and it was good for me. It helped me rebuild my self-confidence and I was able to help people. My light was beginning to shine brighter by the day.

Then what I see as a miracle, I heard back from the MGM and was offered a job as a spa coordinator. Wow, I thought. I was so happy and proud that I was moving forward with my life. The job was going to be at the Excalibur Hotel and Casino. I had to wait almost 2 months before the job would be available for me, but it was mine!

Chapter 16
The One!

One night I had a dream about my one true love. In my dream, I saw his sparkling aqua blue eyes, high cheekbones, dark hair and warm smile. I could almost feel his soft skin. He would be my eagle, my warrior and prince. It gave me a weird and comforting feeling at the same time, because he was not the type of man I usually liked. I usually preferred a man that had dark brown eyes with dark hair. But, I knew that God had a plan for me with this blue-eyed man and I knew that I needed to find him. I knew that I couldn't wait around for him to find me. After I awoke from my dream, I wrote a poem about him.

What will it take?

What will it take?
To be real and not fake
What will it take?
To find someone who wants what I want
What I want is not asking a lot
It's just a straight up shot
A straight up shot
At love and happiness
One mate, one passion, a once in a lifetime

I have to wonder is that real?

Or is it me?

Is it something I feel?

I'm broken I'm torn up

I've been to hell and back

And from that I take the good

I've learned a lot

Yet I'm still young

I'm ready and willing

To take a straight shot

A shot at love

As I am a Dove

I believe in love

My man is an Eagle

Eagles fly with Doves

Together we will be each other's flames forever

And desire one another

And together the two of us

Will make three

We will be a family

God will plant the seed

For a new family tree

While waiting for my job, I decided to pursue my dream of one! As I knew what he looked like from my dream, I began to look for him. I wanted to be with my one true love, my soul mate, and my twin flame. He would be my one person in the world that would love me unconditionally and protect me. He would go to church with me and we would feel God's love together.

As I had very little money to buy food for myself, going out and searching for him was out of the question. I needed to find him with as little cost as possible. Joining an on-line dating service was not my thing, but I was lead to it by God. During the process of putting myself back together I had time to find myself. It was important for me to find myself first because if I didn't love myself, how could anyone else truly love me. As I began to meet guys on this site, many of them tried to get to know me. It was good for me to have several men respond to my page as it helped show me that I was still attractive to other men. However, I refused their advances because I wasn't looking for Mr. Right Now, I was looking for Mr. Right!

If I had been desperate it would've been easy to find a quick fix, a band-aid to save me. With plenty of offers it was not my intent to waste my time or theirs, as I knew exactly what I was looking for. I needed to keep my focus on the goal of finding him no matter what or how long it would take. Needing to get out in the real world, I did however go on several dates. They were always in public places and we met there. I knew that I needed to be protective of myself.

I believe that life is about enduring pain. Every one will endure pain in their lives and we learn from the loss and mistakes. It is how we learn to live and love. My life has been tragic with silver linings of triumph. I have endured some very tuff pain, physical and emotional. I have lived a lot of life learning hard lessons along the way. I grew stronger by keeping the focus on my strengths and not my weaknesses.

One evening I lit all of my white candles. They were white because it is a pure and innocent color. I began playing Christian music from church. It was beautiful and peaceful. That was medicine for my soul. I fell to my knees and began praying to God and Jesus. I told them I felt that I had endured enough pain and that I was ready for my true love to come to me. Talking from my heart to Jesus was something I always did, because Jesus really knows who I am and my intent. My intent is pure with kindness and compassion for others.

That night Jesus spoke back to me. It felt like he was right there in my room with me. I was told to go to the computer, which I did. I pulled up the site and began looking at more pictures. Face after face I continued to look and then a miracle! There on the computer screen in front of me was the face I had seen in my dream. I sat frozen and wide-eyed staring at the picture. It was a moment I will never forget. The aqua blue eyes were captivating and his smile was genuine. He was sitting in a chair outdoors with a blue and white shirt on.

At last my search was over. I sat there for several more minutes thinking about what to write in an e-mail to him. After typing and deleting several messages, I sent an e-mail to him and put it in God's hands. Garret and I began talking on the computer for several days and then exchanged phone numbers and set up a time to talk.

As the time of his call approached, I began to get nervous, as I knew this was the man that God had put here for me. Then right on time the phone rang. My nerves went through the roof and my heart began to pound in my chest. I took a deep breath and picked up the phone. It was him, my one and his voice was strong, soft and kind at one time.

We talked for almost three hours and it felt like we already knew each other. The conversation was easy and comfortable with no times where the conversation went flat. He told me about his life and all about himself. I learned all about him, he had a boat and loved going out to Lake Mead and just relaxing. It was his was to keep his sanity. Being on the water was his peaceful getaway. He was a big NFL and NASCAR fan. His favorite team was the Philadelphia Eagles, which I thought was funny as he was my Eagle. He was a real down to earth guy that was looking for his best friend and partner for life. He had never been married and had no children. He had his life in order and was looking for the one person that he wanted to grow old with. I couldn't believe what I was hearing. It was exactly what I was looking for.

I also told him about my life. He listened to my journey and struggles of my life. Not once did he ever judge me or make me feel guilty. He was compassionate and understanding of my pains. Our lives were so different, however we found comfort in each other's path. We were friends first and took it slow. We were both looking for our best friend.

After several conversations over the next few days, which were all several hours long, we decided to meet at a restaurant near my place as we lived on opposite sides of town. When I walked into the restaurant, I immediately saw him sitting at a table facing the door. He recognized me and stood up and took several steps towards me. As we came face to face with each other, we each saw the other person for what they really were. I was very happy with what I saw even though he was not the type of man I usually would go after. I felt that he liked what he saw as well. He was smiling from ear to ear just as I was.

We sat in the restaurant for a few hours just talking and getting to know each other. It was a dream comes true. Here I was with a kind man that was interested in me just as I was interested in him. We each felt quite comfortable talking to each other even though he told me that he is very shy. I didn't see it and thought he was joking with me. As my time with him grew, I realized that he is shy. But he was very comfortable with me and we both knew it was a sign that we were supposed to be together.

Even though I knew he was the one, I still kept him at a safe distance. I felt inadequate as I was in the process of the rest of my life. I was planting seeds for my future and needed them to be safe and nurtured. I didn't want to get thrown back into a life of abuse with a different man. I needed to be sure that he was Mr. Right! I had all the feelings for him. I would think about him all day and night. I wanted to tell him about my dream, but knew that it would probably scare him away forever. So I kept it secret for now.

He invited me out several times when he was going places with his friends. I never showed up and that made him upset. I wanted to be alone with him. He later told me that he wanted me to meet his friends and for several reasons. One was to help me meet more nice people. The other was so that I would feel more comfortable being out with him.

He continued to try and get me out of my shell. Being patient with me, he understood that I was a work in progress. Most important to me was the fact that he knew about my past and disabilities and wasn't discouraged or swayed by them. He accepted me as I was and didn't try to change me. What God gave me was my best friend, my once in a lifetime. He became my biggest fan, the one that cheered me on to the finish line.

On Christmas Eve 2006, He called and invited me over to his house. I was happy that he invited me, as I was in my apartment alone with no Christmas spirit. His call and invitation immediately put me in the Christmas spirit. The entire way over to his house I was listening to and singing Christmas songs.

We sat and talked for a few hours and it was very comforting to me. Here I was in his house alone with him and there were no feelings of fear. At this moment I knew that he was the one. When he walked me to my car, he asked me if he could hold my hand. I said, "Yes!" and he gently reached over and held my hand as he slowly walked me to my car. When we arrived at my car, he gave me a warm hug. Then he helped me get in and closed the door. I rolled down the window and we said our "Goodbyes" as he told me to call him when I was home. I asked him "Why?"

He responded, "So that I know you made it there OK." This reassured my feelings that he was the one. This was the beginning of forever. He stood there and watched me drive away, waving to me until I turned the corner and was out of site.

We overcame the obstacles of a relationship. Living on different sides of town, the drive was about 25 minutes with no traffic. It was fairly easy to deal with to know that we would be in each other's arms shortly. Another problem was that he worked from 4 am until 12 noon and his sleep habits were awkward. This was difficult to learn and work around, but we managed. When we were together it was all worth it as we looked into each other's eyes and could see into our souls. It was as though all of my dreams were coming true. I was so grateful and humble to God for this blessing.

The one thing we didn't seem to have in common was faith. His faith was broken due to disappointment in his youth. I made my faith clear from the start but never forced my faith on him. I spoke of being "evenly yoked" is the only way a marriage or relationship can survive. The magic and miracles in my life opened up his eyes and he began to get to know God again. To my surprise, he began to go to church with me. That was very important to me. Now here I was sitting in church with my one sitting right beside me holding my hand and singing with the band.

We became evenly yoked as Garret put his life in God's hands and was water baptized at Mountain View Christian Church, also called "The Champion Center". Closer and closer we grew, our relationship became stronger. Garret taught me how to laugh again. Not only at myself, but everything. He also taught me to relax not to be too serious all the time. I needed to learn how to stop and enjoy the moment and he did just that.

I began working my new job in January 2007. I was never trained to do this job. The manager must have thought I already knew. So, I basically winged it using my knowledge from working as a nail tech. The manager liked my positive attitude and told me that he hoped it would spread throughout the spa.

Working full time was hard. One thing I enjoyed about this job was that I had to multi-task. It made it challenging and exciting. A bad thing with this job was that I had to stand up all day and with my disabilities this was difficult. But I needed a job and I was going to do my best.

The first month was good, I was getting the place down and it was running better every day. Then it took a turn for the worst. The manager began to pick on me for little things and he quickly turned it personal. Every time I did something good, he would turn it around and scold me for it. This affected my health as I began to break out in hives again. The hive plagued me again and the stress was becoming too much for me to handle. I think he started to become threatened by me for some reason. Probably the fact that he was new to the spa, he transferred from the front desk. They are two totally different departments and cannot be run the same way. I was not permitted to leave the front desk unless there was another person there to cover me. As I was the only person there for the first 5 hours of my shift meant I had to hold it. I couldn't handle the way I was being treated at work and tried to get help from the Personnel Department to no avail. With my health at risk I quit my job and applied for disability.

Garret was very compassionate towards me. Knowing my past, he began to get me healthy again. We went to see my doctor and it was nice. This time it was about me getting better, not him getting pain pills. He convinced me that the dentist wasn't that bad and the feeling of being out of pain would be worth any discomfort the dentist might cause. Not having money, he paid for me to have five root canals and two teeth pulled. I hope that one day I can have a beautiful smile, but my hero could not afford for me to get perfect teeth, he could just afford to get me out of pain. For that I am very thankful!

On March 4, 2007, Garret surprised me with a ticket to attend the NASCAR race in Las Vegas with him. It was exciting as I had never been there before. I watched some races with him prior to this, but this was the real thing. While sitting in our seats, the National Anthem was sung and the military jets flew over. Just then, he looked at me and knelt down on one knee and said, "Tami, Will you marry me?"

This made an incredible day even better! I quickly said, "Yes."

Later, I asked him why he asked me at the race and he said, "I wanted it to be something that we both remember for the rest of our lives."

We picked a date of September 27 to get married. I bought a beautiful dress and finally was able to have the wedding I had dreamed of my entire life. It was a beautiful day as we went to the Little White Wedding Chapel and exchanged our vows in a small ceremony.

Shortly after getting married, we went to the beach in California. We both love the beach and the water is cleansing. I also love trees and the natural beauty of the planet. The California coast is a wonderful place to view some of this natural beauty.

After we checked into our room, we decided to go for a walk on the beach, as the sun was getting ready to set. When we arrived at the sand, we took off our shoes to feel the sand under our feet. Hand in hand we stepped onto the sand looking at each other. Our smiles were ear to ear as our feet sunk into the cool sand. Walking slowly together along the water, I paused as I felt that there was something I really needed to do.

I turned towards Garret and gave him a gentle kiss on the lips and asked him to wait there. I turned and began to walk into the water stopping at waist level. The sunset was glimmering off the water in an orange/red glow. Lifting my cross from my neck, I kissed it and said, "Thank You, God." I spread my arms out to the side like they were wings and pulled them towards the front cutting the water and making the water fly into the air. Shedding my old life for my new life at that moment. A content smile emerged across my face as I slowly turned towards the beach. There he was at last, my best friend. I smiled at him and he smiled back at me. We both began to walk towards each other meeting in the middle and we embraced in a kiss full of unconditional love.

In my dream God showed me my one. I knew that when I met him I would know who he was. As always, God was right!

The Intent of the Heart

What is the Intent of the Heart?
I ask myself that Question
Every hour of every day
It is not enough to lift your hands and pray
To make the difference
Someone must first take the stand
And step up to the plate
I am brave enough
I am tough enough
I will walk with Jesus every step of the way
From the line of straightness
I will unfortunately sway
From time to time
And on that one special day
I will lift my hands and cry
Thank You!
Thank you for sending me the one for me

Who has a pure intent of the heart and soul
A tough skinned man
Willing to love just one woman
Enough to last an eternity
Of love and togetherness
We will send out the Doves
And have a child together and forever
Be the parents
That God wants us to be
Forever we will be a family

To be continued......

Summary

Domestic violence is a sad but real part of our society. There are many people that live with abuse everyday because they are scared, alone, think that they are stuck and they have nowhere to turn, or believe that they deserve what they are getting. They do not deserve to be abused, only loved.

Domestic violence has many different forms. It has many different ways of damaging a person or family. It is not just being physically abused it can also be verbal and mental as well. Everyone knows that physical abuse is damaging to a person on the outside, but it also does damage to one's self-respect. Verbal abuse is intended to belittle a person into believing that they are inadequate or unworthy. Making them believe in things that are not true. If someone tells you that you are ugly, over time we begin to believe him or her. When we do, they have a power over us. Everyone must believe in him or herself and most importantly, love themselves no matter what anyone says to them.

Domestic violence is often a learned behavior. Many people grow up in a household where domestic violence is happening. As a child, the children see this and believe that it is a normal part of society. Young boys grow up thinking that it is normal and they in turn do it. Young girls grow up seeing it and think that they are supposed to allow this to happen. They think it happened to my mother so it is supposed to happen to me. It is not supposed to happen to anyone. Everyone must learn and understand that domestic violence is wrong on all fronts. Only then can it be removed from our society.

Drugs and alcohol use can increase the behavior also. When people use drugs or alcohol, they lose some control of their emotions and judgment. A person might not be abusive until they use one of these substances. They can trigger abuse in a normally calm and loving person, but it still doesn't make it right.

If you are a woman that is being abused by your husband, boyfriend or partner, you owe it to yourself to get help and GET OUT! Especially if you have children, your children will eventually be abused also if they are not already being abused. Don't think that the abuse stops with you, it never does. Your children will grow up thinking it is a normal way of life and be abusive towards their partner or allow their partner to be abusive to them. You are their teacher, it is up to you to show them right from wrong and to do that you need to stop the abuse.

If you are a man being abused by a woman, you also owe it to yourself and children to GET OUT! Domestic violence goes both ways. It is not always the man that is abusive. Women can also be the violent party. Men have a belief that they are supposed to be strong and able to control a woman so most men don't report being abused. Men need to get over the stereotype and report the abuse. There is help out there for you as well.

The nightmare of domestic violence you live will not end until you stop the abuse and get help. Getting help is easy, just tell someone, your family, your church, the police, anyone. There are a lot of organizations out there waiting for your call to help you. YOU need to make the call. They will help you and protect you. Tell them what is happening to you. Tell them your fears so that they can understand your position and needs. Don't be afraid. Once you begin to get help, you will have people and resources to help protect you. If you stay in an abusive relationship, eventually you will end up a statistic. No one wants to be a statistic! You are a child of God; what ever your belief is God loves you!